FORBES' VIRGIN ISLANDS CRUISING GUIDE

by
Alexander C. Forbes

PRINTED IN U.S.A.

Dukane Caribbean Books

The Grenadines, Undiscovered Islands of the Caribbean — 243 ...... $6.50
9x12, hard bound, 56 pages with 60 full color pictures by Bruce G. Lynn. A fascinating photographic journey through many little known islands in the West Indies. An informative text relates historical and cultural facts.

Barbados, A Smiling Island — 035 .... $6.50
9x12, hard bound, 56 pages with 55 pictures in full color by Bruce G. Lynn. Masterful photographs of colorful mounted police, cricket matches and English architecture show why this island is often called "Little England." An accompanying text gives an extraordinary insight into the island's history and growth.

The Virgin Islands, Pleasure Spots in the Caribbean — 036 .... $6.50
9x12, hard bound, 56 pages with 60 full color pictures by Bruce G. Lynn. Freeport shopping bazaars, native fishing boats, plantation ruins and glistening hotels form an endless variety of exotic contrasts. A delightful text reveals a colorful history of pirates, wars, conquests and domination.

Yachting Guide to the Grenadines — 027 .... $3.95
6x9, 148 pages, spiral bound, by Donald M. Street, Jr., noted author and Caribbean yachtsman. A must for anyone planning to cruise these fabulous waters. Beautifully illustrated with colorful photographs, line drawings and charts.

Undersea Garden of the Virgin Islands — 034 .... $1.95
6x9, 32 pages with over 55 photographs by Janet Viertel. An underwater photographic tour of Buck Island Reef. Outstanding photographs of colorful schools of tropical fish, unique coral formations and fascinating sea life in this underwater National Park.

Birds of the Virgin Islands — 464 .... $3.95
9x12, 28 pages, 110 full color paintings by Dea Murray. A simplified identification guide to the beautiful birds of the Virgin Islands. A complete description of each bird gives coloring, nesting and feeding habits and voice characteristics.

A Romantic History of St. Croix — 021 .... $3.50
6½x8, hard bound, 72 pages, by Florence Lewisohn. A fascinating account of old plantation days and the story of the sugar and rum industry.

Tales of Tortola and the British Virgin Islands — 022 .... $3.50
6x9, hard bound, 96 pages, by Florence Lewisohn. Recounting nearly five centures of lore, legend and history.

St. Croix Under Seven Flags — 015 .... $8.95
6x9, hard bound, 456 pages. A major historical work by Florence Lewisohn covering the 500 years of recorded island history. Lavishly illustrated with seldom seen reproductions dating from the 1400's to today.

FORBES' VIRGIN ISLANDS CRUISING GUIDE

**written
&
illustrated
by
Alexander C. Forbes**

Published by Dukane Press, Hollywood, Florida

Sketch by Jean Chapman

AUTHOR's NOTE

This publication is not to be considered a Navigational Aid.
It is offered only as a supplement to assist you in choosing a
safe and pleasant anchorage.

Library of Congress Catalog No. 71-142111
ISBN 0-87800-080-1.

CONTENTS

DEDICATED TO
Basil Holmes,
who's unfailing interest and enthusiasm
were major factors in my writing this work.

Sir Francis Drake Channel

AN INTRODUCTION TO THE VIRGIN ISLANDS

The Virgin Islands are a group of generally mountainous islands lying between the Virgin Passage and the Anegada Passage approximately forty miles east of Puerto Rico on the northeastern side of the Caribbean Sea. The chain continues eastward uninterruptedly for forty-five miles.

These islands are owned in part by the United States and Great Britain. The American Virgins include three of the major islands: St. Thomas, St. John and St. Croix as well as approximately 50 other islands and cays, many of which are uninhabited. The British Virgin Islands include Tortola, Virgin Gorda, Anegada, Jost van Dyke and Peter Island as well as approximately 23 smaller islands and cays. A line of demarkation runs from the north to the south between Little Hans Lollik and Little Tobago, through The Narrows between St. John and Great Thatch Island, around the eastern end of St. John and thence through the Flanagan Passage between Flanagan and Pelican Islands. All islands to the westward of this line are American possessions and all islands to the eastward are British.

In the U.S. Virgin Islands the major ports for commerce are Charlotte Amalie on St. Thomas and Christiansted on St. Croix. The major British port is Roadtown, Tortola. Both St. Thomas and St. Croix do a booming tourist business which caters primarily to visitors from the continental United States. Recently this business has begun to overflow into the British Virgin Islands resulting in extensive development in parts of that area.

7

St. Thomas and St. Croix are both well supplied with U.S.-type super-markets, good restaurants and hotels. Tortola, though not nearly so sophisticated as her American sisters, also offers these services in limited degrees of quantity and quality. Shipyards and marine repair facilities are scattered throughout the area offering varying standards of efficiency and service. Marine supply outlets may also be found on these three islands with inventories ranging from sparse to adequate.

We who live in the Virgin Islands feel that this is the most beautiful cruis-ing area in the world. The weather is generally consistent; a comfortable anchorage is available almost every 20 minutes (many of these are safe for overnight stays); the swimming and snorkeling are unsurpassed; and the beaches . . . superb! The fishing is deemed to be the best in the world. This statement is backed up by our annual number of record catches, the most famous of which is the world's record blue marlin caught by local resident, John Battles. The catch was officially weighed in at 865 pounds ! ! ! The previous record, also caught by a Virgin Islander, weighed 814 pounds.

Precautions against tide and/or current activity in all but a few of the many anchorages are unnecessary (see text on the individual anchorages). The wind is generally consistent, blowing from the east. During the winter these trade winds usually blow slightly north of east and can reach veloci-ties of 18 to 22 knots with gusts as high as 40. During the summer they usually veer slightly south of east and decrease in intensity to around 12 to 15 knots with gusts of 25 to 30.

The seas in Pillsbury Sound and the Sir Francis Drake Channel (the major cruising areas of the Virgin Islands) seldom exceed 2 to 3 feet even under the heaviest conditions except where locally affected by tidal streams. Once away from the protection of the islands, however, the seas can build to formidable size. The passage between St. Croix and the main Virgin Islands complex should therefore be considered carefully when a fresh breeze is blowing. Also the Virgin Passage and the Anegada Passage can become quite uncomfortable and should only be attempted by the experienced sailor.

Happily, however, the major cruising grounds of the Virgin Islands are the protected waters of Pillsbury Sound and the Sir Francis Drake Channel. This guide deals primarily with anchorages located in these lovely areas. Not all of the anchorages shown on the sketch charts are good overnight anchorages, so it is extremely important that care be taken in reading the accompanying text.

CUSTOMS & IMMIGRATION

U.S. REGULATIONS:
All vessels must "clear" and "enter" through U.S. Customs and Immigra-tion when leaving and entering U.S. waters. This can be done at either

Cruz Bay, St. John; Charlotte Amalie, St. Thomas; or Christiansted, St. Croix, during normal working hours on week-days and until 12 noon on Saturdays. Any other time will be considered as overtime and a substantial overtime charge can be expected. The Cruz Bay inspectors are ONLY available during normal working hours.

EXCEPTIONS to the above:
1.) American flag vessels that are Coast Guard numbered need not "clear" American waters provided that:
   a.) There are no aliens on board.
   b.) The vessel is not carrying passengers for hire.

2.) American flag vessels that are U.S. Customs Yacht Documented need not "clear" American waters provided that:
   a.) There are no aliens on board.
   b.) The vessel is not carrying passengers for hire.

Any vessel dealing in trade or a commercial venture is required to "clear". ALL vessels are required to "enter".

BRITISH REGULATIONS:
ALL vessels must "enter" and "clear" through British Customs and Immigration when entering and leaving British waters. This can be done during normal working hours (as above) at Roadtown and West End, Tortola, and usually at Great Harbor, Jost van Dyke. There is also an inspector at Anegada as well as Virgin Gorda; but they are sometimes hard to find. We recommend West End.

A vessel not engaged in trade or any commercial venture and planning to spend not more than 48 hours in British waters may "enter" and "clear" simultaneously at the discretion of the Customs Officer.

Sketch by Jean Chapman

CHARTS

The following charts are recommended for use as navigational aids for the area described in this guide:

AMERICAN:

U.S. Coast & Geodetic Survey:
> #905: Virgin Islands overall chart
> 933: St. Thomas Harbor chart
> 938: Pillsbury Sound Chart
> 935: Christiansted Harbor

U.S. Navy Hydrographic Office:
> #137: Road Harbor and Approaches
> 569: Gorda Sound and Approaches
> 3904: Tortola to Anegada

BRITISH ADMIRALTY CHARTS:
> #2452: Tortola to Culebra
> 2019: Tortola to Virgin Gorda
> 2008: Anegada to Virgin Gorda
> 2183: St. Thomas Harbor
> 485: St. Croix
> 2020: Road Harbor and Approaches
> 2016: Approaches to Gorda Sound

RADIO FREQUENCIES

The following are the SHIP-TO-SHORE radio frequencies which are used most frequently in the Virgin Islands:

> 2638: The "Children's Hour" is on this frequency every day from NOON to about 1:00 PM. At this time all charterboats in the area pass messages. Also during this time shore facilities in the British Virgins such as Marina Cay, Drakes Anchorage and Tortola Yacht Services stand by for dinner reservations, service orders, etc.
>
> 2182: Coast Guard. Also St. Thomas Marine Operator stands by.
>
> 2678: Coast Guard Auxiliary.
>
> 2009: Operating frequency of the St. Thomas Marine Operator, WHISKY ALPHA HOTEL, and is on the air from 8:00 AM to 9:00 PM. They can patch into the telephone system and will also relay messages to shore facilities in the British Virgins.

SWIMMING HAZARDS

The waters around the Virgin Islands are generally clear, warm and delightful for swimming. Marine hazards are much the same here as in any tropical area and present little problem so long as the following common-sense rules are observed:

SHARKS:

There are sharks in these waters but most of them are offshore on the 100-fathom curve where food is plentiful. You will most certainly not be bothered by sharks (and probably not even see one) if you follow these basic rules:

    1.) NEVER SWIM when garbage has been thrown into the water.
    2.) NEVER SWIM when there is blood of any kind in the water.
    3.) NEVER SWIM when the water is murky.
    4.) NEVER SWIM after sunset or before sunrise.

BARRACUDA:

There are lots of barracuda down here, but if you observe the above rules you should experience no problems with them. Barracudas are very curious fish and will follow you around just to see what you are doing. Don't shoot barracuda with a spear gun unless you're ready for a fight. Leave them alone and they'll leave you alone.

SEA URCHINS:

These spiny creatures will undoubtedly be your most dangerous underwater enemy. They are usually found on coral sand bottoms and around coral reefs. Always look for sea urchins in the water before going swimming and stay out of their reach. Sea urchin barbs can go through the rubber sole of a shoe and once embedded in your flesh cannot be easily removed.

CORAL:

Avoid rubbing against coral when swimming. There are some species of this marine life that can cause considerable pain when touched, so if you're not sure . . . stay clear.

CURRENT, TIDES, TIDAL STREAMS and ROLLERS

CURRENT

The current runs from east to west at a speed of ½ to 1 knot. Its direction and velocity, however, can be greatly affected by tidal streams and wind. Generally speaking the current usually increases slightly as the wind increases from the east; though only in certain isolated areas does it ever exceed 1½ knots. Conversely, there are certain areas where the current is considerably lighter. Example: when sailing east along the south coast of St. Thomas, it is always beneficial to stay close to shore as the current here is substantially less and the seas easier than those found when standing out.

TIDES

The phenomena of tides in the Virgin Islands have been a source of contention throughout the years. The British Admiralty Pilot states that we experience the standard two tides daily, while their charts mention a diurnal condition (see Admiralty Chart #2016). The American Pilot, on the other hand, informs us that a diurnal condition prevails on the Caribbean side only and a semi-diurnal condition is found on the Atlantic side. Tide tables for the Virgin Islands are based on tides in San Juan, Puerto Rico, for the north side of the islands and Galveston, Texas, for the south side. Needless to say, these tables are not too accurate. Tides have been known to flow in the same direction for days at a time in certain areas under very strong wind conditions.

Happily, however, the standard rise and fall of the tide is only 10 to 16 inches . . . not really much of a problem.

For those wishing to explore this further the following rule is said to be given by a local fisherman (I found it in an 1863 Pilot) and is the most interesting I have come across:

RULE: "From the moon's rising until her meridian passage, the flood runs to the southeastward or to windward; and from thence to her setting the ebb runs to the northwestward or to leeward, and vice versa with the lower transit; hence there is a 6-hour stream each way. This rule, however, is greatly interfered with in different localities as well as by the force and direction of the wind. It is observed that the southern tide predominates during the summer months from the middle of June to the middle of August, and two tides have been known to follow in succession, particularly if the wind has been westerly. On such occasions the perpendicular rise has been increased by two feet. Near the commencement of this remarkable change the stream is observed to set for 8 or 10 days continually to the southward with a force seldom surpassed and is called by the fishermen 'St. John's Tide' from its occurring near the day of that Saint. For the remainder of the above period, the ebb or northerly stream will run for about one or two hours. During the months of September, November, March and April, the northern tide prevails with considerable force being assisted by the current. At this period the highest water is generally in the morning and there is usually only a half tide in the evening. The reverse takes place during the summer months.

"The establishment for high water at full and change appears to be about 9h0m, but it is liable to great uncertainty, for sometimes it is as early as 7h0m. The rise and fall at springs is from a foot to a foot and a half, but in the months of April and May the mean level of the sea is observed to be a foot lower than at other periods.

"The duration of the stream (as before stated) is 6 hours each way, and to which the stranger must pay strict attention, leaving the time of high water as a thing of minor importance.

"As already observed, the northern stream is called the flood and that coming from the southward is called the ebb. Strictly speaking, however, this may be an error, although not of much consequence; for the change of set takes place at about half tide on the shore and, the rise and fall being so small, it is difficult to say to which set the term 'flood' should be applied.

"It happens, however, that the commencement of the flood stream takes place at full and change at about 6h0m and runs for 6 hours before it changes to ebb. By remembering this establishment for the first beginning of flood, the turn of the tide can be calculated for any intermediate day during lunation. As 6h0m happens to be nearly the time of the moon's rising at full and change, we have the fisherman's rule explained."

Unfortunately the exact position in the Virgin Islands where this rule applies was not given . . .

TIDAL STREAMS

There are numerous tidal streams running in various directions throughout the Virgin Islands complex. These sometimes drastically affect both the direction and strength of the prevailing current. **The Narrows** offers a good example of tidal stream effect on current: when the flood tide is running (north to south) a tidal stream funnels through Thatch Cut and runs directly across The Narrows. Turning eastward along the St. John shoreline this stream follows the contours of the island and finally flows into the Caribbean through the Flanagan Passage. During this condition a current in excess of two knots can be found close to the St. John shore; while a light westerly current, or none at all, will be found along the Tortola shore. Therefore, a yacht sailing eastward through The Narrows in a flood tide will certainly benefit by staying close to the St. John shoreline, while one making a west-bound passage would do well to hug the Tortola side.

ROLLERS

This is a formidable type of ground swell which frequently occurs from October to May and sometimes continues for three or four days in succession. These Rollers generally move in from the northward after several days of light east to southeasterly winds. They have been observed to obtain heights in excess of 6 feet and have been seen to top and break in 9 fathoms of water off the northern coast of Tortola. In some places near the western end of Anegada where the bottom is composed of fine sand, the formation of banks is frequently changed by these Rollers. Great care should therefore be taken in anchoring in any harbors exposed to the north during these winter months. BEWARE: several yachts have come to grief in recent years because their skippers either ignored or were unaware of this hazard. All anchorages listed in this guide which could, in the author's opinion, experience this phenomenon will be so labeled in their written descriptions . . . read carefully! ! !

Sketch by Jean Chapman

MARINAS

Marinas in the Virgin Islands are limited both in number and quality at the present time. There are, however, improvements planned for some of these plus several new marinas under construction which we hope will relieve the situation within the next year or two.

ST. THOMAS can presently boast of only five such establishments which show any resemblance to the average yachtsman's concept of the word "marina". Only limited dockage is available for transients, so any request for space should be made well in advance of arrival. Those wishing further information may obtain same from the marinas themselves, which are listed below:

> **YACHT HAVEN MARINA** is the largest on the island having over 100 berths. Its location is in Long Bay, the easternmost area of the main harbor. Dockmaster, Capt. Bob Smith, has informed me that all slips are presently filled with an extensive waiting list for vacancies. However, ample mooring room is available in the harbor and Bob can always accommodate transient yachts along-side for short periods. We understand that an expansion program is presently in the works which will extend the capacity of the facility to 350 slips. The marina is a popular stop for yachtsmen because of the three supermarkets which lie within easy walking distance of the dock. The town center is only 5 minutes away by taxi. For further information contact:
>
> Capt. Bob Smith, Dockmaster
> Yacht Haven Marina
> St. Thomas, V.I. 00801
> Tel: 774-6050
>
> **AVERY's BOATHOUSE, INC.** is located on the western side of the main harbor in the Frenchtown area, only a five-minute taxi ride from the center of Charlotte Amalie. A slight "down-east" atmosphere prevails around this quaint, family operation. Dick Avery, President, delegates the necessary authority to get the work done (even does a little himself now and then) while wife, Marianne, gets on with the business of running a very substantial bare-boat charter operation. The pace is relaxed and friendly. For further information contact:
>
> Dick Avery
> Avery's Boathouse, Inc.
> P.O. Box 2393
> St. Thomas, V.I. 00801
> Tel: 774-0111
>
> **LAGOON MARINA** is located at Red Hook on the eastern end of the island. This is a powerboat haven for fishing enthusiasts run by Capt. Johnny Harms, who is recognized as the best fishing guide in the

Caribbean. Sailing boats are also welcome. Johnny has built this marina complex from scratch and is doing an excellent job in continuing the expansion. The marina is normally a 30-minute drive from the town center. Unfortunately, taxis are hard to find in the evening (if none are around, try calling tthe East End Taxi Service). However, for drug and food supplies, a small shopping center with a supermarket is located at Ft. Milner, which is only a 10-minute drive toward town. For further information contact:

Capt. Johnny Harms
Lagoon Marina
Red Hook
St. Thomas, V.I. 00801
Tel: 774-0570

LAGOON FISHING CENTER (not to be confused with the Lagoon Marina) is located in the Lagoon on the southeastern end of the island. This marina is beautifully protected from any type of foul weather by its secluded position in a mangrove backwater. Unfortunately the approach is narrow, winding and quite shallow. Only boats drawing 5 feet or less can safely negotiate this entrance. We understand, however, that a plan is in the works for dredging the channel to a respectable depth. This marina caters primarily to the sport fishing crowd though sailing boats are certainly welcome. For further information contact:

Capt. Jerry Black
Estate Frydenhoj
St. Thomas, V.I. 00801
Tel: 774-4444

ANTILLES YACHTING CORPORATION is located in the mangrove lagoon on the southeastern end of the island. This brand new facility was just begun in the spring of 1969 and already shows promise of being one of the best in the area. Catering primarily to marine hauling and bare-boat charter, the operators also have plans for a lovely marina complex as well as a marine store and possible bar/restaurant. The dockage is presently limited, though owner-operator, Tom Kelly, assured me that he would always find room for transient yachtsmen. Unfortunately the entrance channel restricts yacht draft to 5 feet or less, though Tom claims that an excess of 6 feet can be brought to the dock in the right tide conditions. If you're planning to use this facility and draw over 5 feet, I suggest you ask Tom to personally guide you in. Plans for dredging this channel are presently being studied by the government and approval is expected momentarily. For further information contact:

Tom Kelly
P.O. Box 721
St. Thomas, V.I. 00801
Tel: 774-5096 or 774-1503

15

TORTOLA has plans for several vast new marina complexes which hopefully will be developed within the next few years. Presently, however, Tortola Yacht Services is the only facility where the expected marina services can be obtained.

> **TORTOLA YACHT SERVICES** is located at Ft. Burt in the southwestern corner of Road Harbor. The facility is run by Alby Stewart, a very friendly guy who is always ready to help visiting yachtsmen. Though the slips are almost always full, transient yachts can usually find a stern-to position at the fuel dock. The facility is just a short cab ride or walk from the center of Roadtown and is by far the most pleasant anchorage in Road Harbor. A lovely new pub next door and the best hotel on the island just across the street add to the attraction of this marina. For further information contact:
>
> > Alby Stewart
> > Tortola Yacht Services
> > Roadtown, Tortola
> > B.V.I.
> > Tel: Tortola 2124

VIRGIN GORDA, like Tortola, has plans for several marinas. The only one of these presently in operation is the Little Dix Bay Marina, which is a godsend for those wishing to visit Spanish Town, The Baths, or Little Dix Bay Resort.

> **LITTLE DIX BAY MARINA** is being developed by Rockresorts Inc. of New York, who operate both the Caneel Bay Plantation on St. John and the Little Dix Bay Resort on Virgin Gorda. The marina is located in the protection of the saltwater marsh just off St. Thomas Bay. This facility will eventually be able to accommodate yachts up to 100 feet in length. Plans for the complex include complete yacht facilities, a restaurant/bar as well as a possible hotel. The project is scheduled for completion in mid-1971, though slips for a limited number of yachts are presently available. We are very pleased about this development, because everything Rockresorts has done in the Virgin Islands has been of top quality, and we're sure this will be also. For further information contact:
>
> > E. David Brewer, General Manager
> > Little Dix Bay
> > P.O. Box 5109
> > St. Thomas, V.I. 00801
> > Tel: Virgin Gorda 233

ST. CROIX. There are several hotels on the waterfront in Christiansted Harbor which have limited dockage available. Examples of these are the Old Quarter, the Kings Alley Hotel and the Comanche. These, however, cannot be considered "marinas" because of the limited facilities that they offer; their docks being merely a convenience for their guests. Because of their location right in town, these hotel docks are in great demand, and obtaining a slip on one is considered a feat of no small proportion. The St. Croix Marine & Development Corp, though located slightly out of town, is the only marina in St. Croix where the expected services can be found.

ST. CROIX MARINE & DEVELOPMENT CORP. is located in Gallows Bay on the eastern side of Christiansted Harbor. The primary function of this operation in the past has been marine hauling, repair and sales. Recently, however, owner, Bill Chandler, decided to install more dockage and set up a proper marina. There are presently 36 slips complete with water, power, etc. Transients only are permitted to live aboard. For further information contact:

> Bill Chandler
> St. Croix Marine & Development Corp.
> P.O. Box 1149
> Christiansted, St. Croix 00820
> Tel: 773-0289

Sketch by Jean Chapman

MARINAS (see text for additional information)

NAME	DEPTH AT DOCK	FUEL	WATER	POWER	TOILETS	SHOWER	ICE	LIVE ABOARD	No. OF SLIPS	RESTAU- RANT	BAR
ST. THOMAS											
YACHT HAVEN MARINA	12	yes	yes	110/ 220	yes	yes	yes	yes	100	yes	yes
BOATHOUSE	20	planned for the future	yes	110/ 220	yes	yes	yes	yes	40	no	yes
LAGOON MARINA	8	yes	yes	110	yes	yes	yes	yes	70	presently closed	
LAGOON FISHING CENTER	5	yes	yes	110/ 220	yes	no	yes	no	38	beer and sandwiches	
ANTILLIES YACHTING CORP.	5		yes		yes	yes	yes	yes	20	no	no
ST. CROIX											
ST. CROIX MARINE AND DEVELOPMENT	12	yes	yes	110/ 220	yes	yes	yes	yes	36	no	no
TORTOLA											
TORTOLA YACHT SERVICES	7	yes	yes	110	yes	yes	yes	yes	30	next door	
VIRGIN GORDA											
LITTLE DIX BAY	12	yes	yes	110/ 220	yes	yes	yes	yes	30-100	soon	soon

SHIPYARDS

The increasing demand for marine maintenance and repair services has created a budding industry long overdue in this area; shipyards are beginning to spring up throughout the islands. Most of these facilities are reasonably well managed and operate relatively new, or at least newly installed, equipment. We do recommend, however, that you make a personal inspection of these facilities prior to deciding which to use.

Name, Location and Telephone No.	Type of Lift	Max. Draft/Beam	Max. Tons	Contract Requirements	Marine Supplies Available
Avery's Boathouse, Inc. Frenchtown St. Thomas Tel.: 774-0111 Mailing Address: P.O. Box 2393, St. Thomas	Inclined Railway	8 / 15	30	Boathouse will supply both labor and materials or you can supply both yourself.	Woolsey Paint and a few other items.
Island Yachts, Inc. Yacht Haven St. Thomas Tel.: 774-3000 Mailing Address: P.O. Box 1512, St. Thomas, V.I.	Floating Drydock	6½ / 18	20+	You can do your own work only if you haul on weekends and holidays.	Complete.
West Indian Company, Ltd. West Indian Co. Dock St. Thomas Tel.: 774-1780 Mailing Address: Same	Crane Operated Sling	5½ / —	20	You must supply all your own labor and materials.	Carpentry shop sells paint.
Antillies Yachting Corp. Mangrove Lagoon East End of St. Thomas Tel.: 774-5096 or 774-1503 Mailing Address: P.O. Box 721, St. Thomas, V.I.	Travel-Lift	5 / 15	30+	Yard will supply both labor and materials, or you may supply both.	Complete.
St. Croix Marine & Development Corp. Gallows Bay, St. Croix Tel.: 773-0289 Mailing Address: P.O. Box 1149, Christiansted, St. Croix	Inclined Railway	10 / 20	60+	Yard reserves the right to do all the work from gunnel to gunnel under the keel.	Complete.
Tortola Yacht Services Ft. Burt Roadtown, Tortola Tel.: 2124 Mailing Address: Same	Inclined Railway	6½ / 22	40	You can only do your own work on the bottom if you haul on weekends or holidays.	Complete.

MARINE SUPPLY STORES

Local demand has fostered the development of several quite comprehensive marine stores in the area. Shipyards are also capitalizing on the demand by opening small stores in conjunction with their maintenance and repair facilities. These stores are listed below along with one or two sporting goods and hardware shops which supply related equipment.
In St. Thomas

> **SEA SAGA ENTERPRISES,** probably the most comprehensive marine store in the Virgin Islands, carries everything from paint to flags. It is located on the waterfront right next to Palm Passage. Tel: 774-0080

> **BOSUNS LOCKER** is a branch of Sea Saga located at Yacht Haven. Tel: 774-1696

> **AVERY's BOATHOUSE INC.** located in Frenchtown carries Woolsey paint plus a limited assortment of other supplies such as Seaboard fittings, diving gear, Sunfish (and parts), etc. Tel: 774-0111

> **ANTILLES YACHTING CORP.** located in the mangrove lagoon on the eastern end of the island, carries Woolsey paint as well as Seagull outboards (and parts) and various other supplies. They plan to expand their inventory considerably during the coming year. Tel: 774-5096 or 774-1503

> **LAGOON MARINA,** located at Red Hook on the eastern end of the island, carries various marine items plus fishing tackle and related gear. Tel: 774-0570

> **C & M CARON** on Mainstreet in Charlotte Amalie has a very complete sporting goods department where a large choice of fishing and diving gear is available. Tel: 774-2220

> **FRANCOIS HARDWARE,** on the waterfront just west on the International Plaza, is a good spot for buying chain, galvanised shackles and such at a much better price than usually found in the marine stores. Tel: 774-2370

In St. Croix

> **THE SEA SHOP,** in the Pan American Arcade, Christiansted, carries a good line of paints as well as other marine supplies and hardware. Tel: 773-1229

> **ST. CROIX MARINE & DEVELOPMENT CORPORATION,** in Gallows Bay just outside of Christiansted, has a very comprehensive marine store which handles a wide range of paints, hardware, and other related marine supplies. Tel: 773-0289

In Tortola

> **TORTOLA YACHT SERVICES,** located at Ft. Burt in Roadtown, is the first and foremost marine store in the British Virgin Islands. Though not as complete as the St. Thomas and St. Croix supply houses, this facility has an ample stock (most of the time) of the necessary items as well as a surprising variety of other gear. They also carry a good

size inventory of Mercury outboard, inboard, and outdrive parts as well as other engine parts and accessories. Tel: 2124

SUPERMARKETS, FOOD & LIQUOR SUPPLY STORES

ST. THOMAS has the largest selection of food and liquor stores in the Virgin Island complex. There are stores operated by two major supermarket chains plus numerous smaller markets located within walking distance of the main harbor. Three of the largest supermarkets are within two blocks of Yacht Haven. Liquor can be purchased in all supermarkets or in the numerous liquor stores located throughout the town. Liquor prices are approximately the same everywhere. For yachtsmen anchored on the eastern end of the island there is a supermarket in the Ft. Milner Shopping Center, just a short taxi drive from Red Hook. Case lots of liquor, canned and bottled goods as well as frozen meats may also be purchased from several wholesale outlets on the outskirts of town. Addresses and telephone numbers of all these merchants may be found in the local telephone directory.

ST. CROIX's facilities are much the same as those in St .Thomas, though not quite so comprehensive. The main shopping center is Christiansted. Fredricksted has more limited, but quite adequate, shopping facilities.

ST. JOHN: the town of Cruz Bay has several small food and liquor dealers. Most of the food is canned and the choice is limited.

TORTOLA at the present time has no supermarket, though one is in the planning stage. Limited supplies of fresh and frozen meats and vegetables may, however, be obtained in Roadtown. Canned and bottled goods are plentiful. The prices for food are higher in Roadtown than in the American Virgin Islands, so it is wise to do most of your shopping in St. Thomas.

ICE

Ice in cube form can be purchased at all the marinas listed. Block ice may be obtained at either The Boathouse in St. Thomas or the ice plants themselves in Charlotte Amalie, Christiansted or Roadtown. Quality of the block ice varies from good to poor. If you are buying from the ice plant in Charlotte Amalie bear in mind that the St. Thomas taxi drivers are reluctant to carry ice because it gets their trunks wet. In Tortola they don't seem to mind.

FISHING

The Virgin Islands offer some of the best game fishing in the world. There are professional fishing guides and deep sea fishing boats available for charter in St. Thomas, St. Croix and Tortola. The man primarily responsible for the development is world famous Capt. Johnny Harms, who now makes his home in St. Thomas and operates a marina facility on the eastern end of the island.

Johnny was originally brought to the islands by Lawrence Rockefeller to skipper his deep sea fisherman, Savana Bay, and put the Virgin Islands on the map as one of the greatest game fishing areas in the world. It took him a little over one year to do just that when Elliot Fishman, a local angler, under Harms' direction boated a world record blue marlin which weighed in at 814 pounds. Within another year John Battles, also a local angler and also under the direction of Johnny, boated an even larger blue marlin which weighed in at 845 pounds. This fish presently holds the world record.

Our local waters also abound with such fighting fish as white marlin, wahoo, allison tuna, blackfin tuna, oceanic bonito, tarpon, bonefish and many others.

The good fishing boats are booked well in advance of the season so make your reservations early.

HOTELS, BEACH CLUBS and GUEST HOUSES

There are numerous hotels, guest houses and beach clubs throughout the Virgin Islands with more flinging open their doors every day. We have listed just a few of the nicer ones which we feel would be acceptable to our yachting friends. This list is not necessarily based on cost, though the nicer places usually cost a little more. It is, on the other hand, influenced more by comfort and service, as well as in some instances the proximity to local yachting facilities. These are the places that we would choose if we were coming for a visit. Any reservations should be made well in advance for the winter season. Also, remember that a rental car is a must if you're planning to stay more than a day or two.

ST. THOMAS

BOLONGO BAY BEACH CLUB — located on the south shore of the island on a lovely beach only 10 minutes drive from town, offers efficiency units completely equipped for beach-side living. Manager, Raymond Hasbrouck, is one of the best in the business, and the place shows it.

GALLEON HOUSE — this old West Indian House right in town has a real island flavor. Owners, Marty and Anne Clark, host the establishment beautifully with Marty on the piano in the evening. You might not get to sleep very early, but you're sure to have fun! The food is good too.

ISLAND BEACHCOMBER — on its own sandy beach in Lindbergh Bay is a pleasant, surprisingly quiet spot even though the airport is just across the street. The Bay offers good protection for yachts which can be anchored right off the hotel beach. There is a beach-front bar where breakfast, lunch and cocktails are served; dinner must be found elsewhere.

MAFOLIE HOTEL — on the hillside above Charlotte Amalie. This Mediterranean-type hostelry offers a beautiful panoramic view of both the harbor and the town. Small, casual, informal and unrushed . . . with good food.

PELICAN BEACH CLUB — is situated in its own quiet, secluded cove on the east end of the island. Breakfast is served in your own private patio and the dinner menu is excellent. Just a short distance from the anchorage at Red Hook, this lovely spot offers beautiful views of Pillsbury Sound and the islands to the east.

SHIBUI HOTEL — high on the hill overlooking the airport and the south shore of the island, it is another efficiency complex made up of Japanese style cottages. An informal Tea House serves breakfast, lunch and cocktails. Nice family spot.

ST. CROIX

KINGS ALLEY HOTEL — 22 room hotel located right on the waterfront in Christiansted. Dock, swimming pool, restaurant. Close to all the shops. (773-0103)

KING CHRISTIAN HOTEL — this hotel has 24 rooms, each with its own balcony overlooking the harbor. Swimming pool, restaurant right on the waterfront, bar, etc. (773-1035)

THE LODGE — in the heart of Christiansted. Small, clean, modest rates. Restaurants near by. (773-1535)

OLD QUARTER HOTEL — a new hotel with 25 rooms located right on the waterfront in Christiansted. Pool, restaurant, baby sitters, valet and laundry service. (773-0756)

ST. JOHN

CANEEL BAY PLANTATION — one of the finest hotels in the Caribbean located on the western coast of the island. This resort is the site of an old Danish sugar plantation and is nestled in the scenic beauty of the National Park. Everything is here: lovely beach, tennis courts, nature walks, etc. A well protected yacht anchorage is located right off the hotel beach. The food is reputed to be some of the best in the West Indies.

TORTOLA

FORT BURT HOTEL — is on a bluff just above the Tortola Yacht Services docks and shipyard on the southwestern corner of the main harbor. This modern, attractive hotel offers comfortable accommodations and is only a short walk from town. A good protected yacht anchorage is right across the street.

VIRGIN GORDA

LITTLE DIX BAY — is another first class hotel run by Rockresorts (the Caneel Bay people). This lovely complex is situated on a powdery white beach in its own secluded cove. A beautiful new marina belonging to the resort is only 5 minutes away by cab. Great place to relax.

RESTAURANTS

Dining ashore in the Virgin Islands is generally an informal affair with jackets and ties seldom required. Prices are high so it is important to choose the better places in order to insure satisfaction. Your best bet for finding the best food is to ask local residents; their answers are usually refreshingly honest.

We are listing a few of the restaurants which we have tried and found acceptable. This does not necessarily mean that you will find them so, but at least the odds are with you.

Reservations at all restaurants are a must for dinner. Call before 5 PM.

ST. THOMAS

CAFE BRITTANY — in Creque's Alley between Main Street and the waterfront, is an old warehouse that has been very pleasantly remodeled. Wide variety of seafood and other entrees. Lunch and dinner. (774-5785)

GALLEON HOUSE — is a historic West Indian house located on Government Hill. After dinner combo headed up by owner, Marty Clark, on the piano affords good dancing fun. One-entree menu changes nightly. Good value. Dinner only. Closed Sunday and Monday. (774-1445)

HARBOR VIEW — an elegant 19th century town house overlooking the harbor features Mediterranean cuisine and is excellent for both lunch and dinner. Closed Tuesdays. (774-2651)

MAFOLIE — this interesting villa offers a beautiful view of the harbor area. They specialize in charcoal broiled steaks and lobster. Pleasantly informal. Dinner only. (774-2790)

PELICAN BEACH CLUB — located near Red Hook on the eastern end of the island, this lovely spot has an atmosphere of quiet conviviality and serves very good food. Jackets and ties are required all evenings except Wednesday, when they have a cook-out on the beach. (774-2148)

ST. CROIX

CAFE DE PARIS — located in Kings Alley on the waterfront in Christiansted, this tiny restaurant serves some of the best international cuisine in the Virgin Islands. Lunch and dinner. Closed Sunday. (773-0240)

COMANCHE RESTAURANT — in an open tropical setting on the Christiansted waterfront, this is one of the best restaurants in St. Croix. The seafood is excellent, and so is everything else. Lunch and dinner. (773-2665)

THE STONE BALLOON — one of the most popular eating and drinking spots in Christiansted for yachtsmen as well as locals. Friendly and informal atmosphere. Charcoal broiled steaks and lobster the specialty. Dinner only. Closed Tuesday. (773-0090)

SPRAT HALL — located in Fredricksted, is reputed to be the oldest manor house on the island that has never been destroyed. Built in 1670 it has recently been converted to a guest house. The kitchen is known for its interesting variety of island dishes. Excellent seafood. Congenial atmosphere. Dinner only. (772-0305)

ST. JOHN

CANEEL BAY PLANTATION — pleasant dining in a covered pavillion. Excellent food. Jackets and ties required for dinner. Lunch very informal. (774-1090)

TORTOLA

SIR FRANCIS DRAKE PUB — located right next to Tortola Yacht Services. A handy place for lunch. (2408)

FT. BURT HOTEL — right across the street from Tortola Yacht Services. Offers both lunch and dinner. (2468)

VIRGIN GORDA

LITTLE DIX BAY — like its sister on St. John (the Caneel Bay Plantation) this lovely resort prepares some of the best food in the Caribbean. Jackets are sometimes required. Lunch and dinner. (7233)

Drakes Anchorage   Photo by Jay Stone

(See chart on page 106)

VIRGIN ISLANDS NATIONAL PARK

The Virgin Islands National Park, established December 1, 1956, is administered by the National Park Service, U.S. Department of Interior. This Park encompasses almost two-thirds of St. John and most of the colorful off-shore waters surrounding it. From its mountain trails to its sandy beaches and submerged reefs the Park is open for all to enjoy.

While in Park waters there are several regulations which must be adhered to. Heavy fines are levied against those breaking the rules, so read the following carefully.

FISHING REGULATIONS

1.) Taking of fishes or any other marine life in any way except with rod or line, the rod or line being held in the hand, is prohibited: Provided, that fish may be taken by pots or traps of conventional Virgin Islands design and not larger than five feet at the greatest dimension and bait fish may be taken by nets of no greater over-all length than 20 feet and of mesh not larger than 1 inch stretched.

2.) The use of any type of spearfishing equipment within the boundaries of the Park is prohibited.

Photo by Jay Stone
Anchorage Between Eustatia and Prickely Pear

(See chart on page 109)

27

Virgin Islands National Park
on
St. John

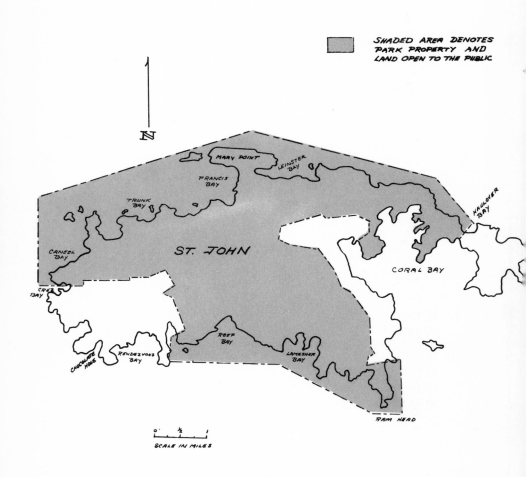

SHADED AREA DENOTES
PARK PROPERTY AND
LAND OPEN TO THE PUBLIC

N

MARY POINT

LEINSTER BAY

FRANCIS BAY

TRUNK BAY

HAULOVER BAY

CANEEL BAY

ST. JOHN

CORAL BAY

CRUZ BAY

REEF BAY

CHOCOLATE HOLE

RENDEZVOUS BAY

LAMESHUR BAY

RAM HEAD

0   ½   1
SCALE IN MILES

3.) Florida Spiny Lobster may be taken by hand or hand held hook. No person shall take female lobsters with eggs; or take more than two lobsters per person per day; or have in possession more than two days' limit.

4.) Species of mollusks commonly known as welks and conchs may be taken by hand. No person shall take more than two conchs or one gallon of welks, or both, per day, or have in possession more than two day's limit.

PROTECTIVE REGULATIONS provide:

1.) No damaging, breaking off, or removing of any underwater growth or formation (coral, sea fans, etc.) or in any other way impairing the natural beauty of the underwater scene (littering, etc.).

2.) The use of anchors must not cause damage to underwater features.

3.) No removing or tampering of wrecks without written permit from the Park Department.

4.) Boats must not be anchored or maneuvered within waters containing marked trails (Trunk Bay Underwater Trail).

5.) Water skiing is not permitted in Park waters.

6.) No fish, offal, bottles, cans, rubbish or other refuse shall be discarded or disposed in Park waters.

7.) All vessels in Park waters shall have a waste receptacle aboard in which all rubbish and refuse shall be deposited.

8.) No person shall discharge or otherwise permit the disposal of toilet wastes within one mile from the nearest shore, unless such wastes are adequately treated by an effective sewage disposal system, including chemical or heat process, which results in disposal of liquid and solid wastes without pollution of the waters.

9.) Cats or dogs are not allowed ashore at Hawksnest, Trunk Bay and Cinnamon Bay. Elsewhere pets must be on a leash at all times.

10.) Do not moor boats to trees or other vegetation ashore.

11.) Keep beaches clean. No beach fires permitted.

Remember: National Park Rangers may at any time board any vessel in Park waters while afloat or underway to examine documents, licenses, or to inspect such vessel to determine compliance with regulations.

For additional information contact the Ranger Stations at Red Hook, Cruz Bay and Lameshur Bay or the Superintendent, Virgin Islands National Park, Box 1707, Charlotte Amalie, St. Thomas, V.I. 00801

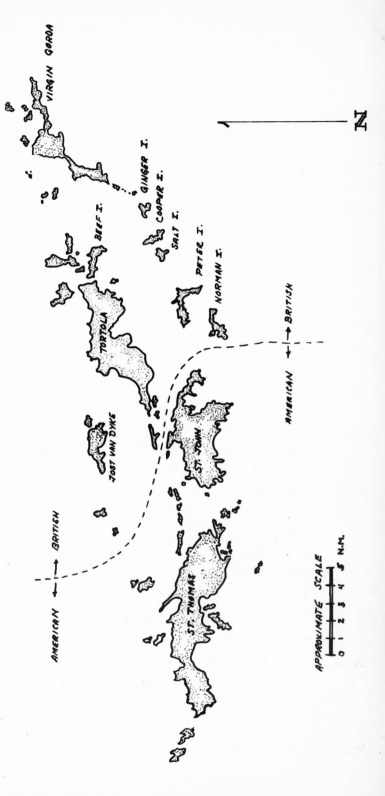

CRUISING GROUNDS
OF
THE VIRGIN ISLANDS
AMERICAN & BRITISH

N

VIRGIN GORDA

GINGER I.
COOPER I.
SALT I.
PETER I.
NORMAN I.
BEEF I.
TORTOLA
JOST VAN DYKE
ST. JOHN
ST. THOMAS

AMERICAN ← → BRITISH
AMERICAN ← → BRITISH

APPROXIMATE SCALE
0 1 2 3 4 5 N.M.

THE US VIRGIN ISLANDS

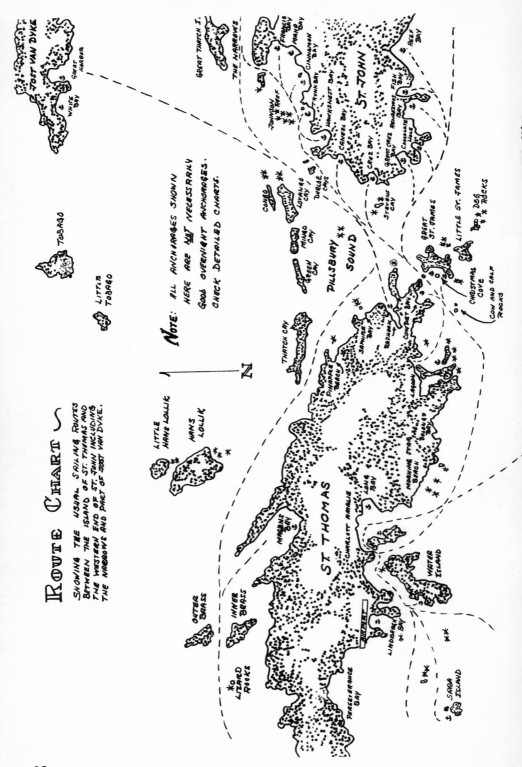

Route Chart ~

Showing the usual sailing routes between the island of St. Thomas and the western end of St. John including the Narrows and part of Jost Van Dyke.

Note: All anchorages shown here are NOT necessarily good overnight anchorages. Check detailed charts.

N

JOST VAN DYKE
GREAT HARBOUR
WHITE BAY

TOBAGO

LITTLE TOBAGO

GREAT THATCH I.
THE NARROWS
FRANCIS ROAD BAY
REEF BAY
FISH BAY
LAMESHUR BAY
CINNAMON BAY
ST. JOHN
THUNK BAY
CANEEL BAY
JOHNSON REEF
CRUZ BAY
GREAT CRUZ BAY
CHOCOLATE HOLE
RENDEZVOUS BAY

CONGO
LOVANGO CAY
DURLOE CAYS
STEVEN CAY
GREAT ST. JAMES
LITTLE ST. JAMES
DOG ROCKS
CHRISTMAS COVE
COW AND CALF ROCKS

GREEN CAY
MINGO CAY

PILLSBURY SOUND

THATCH CAY

LITTLE HANS LOLLIK
HANS LOLLIK

SABA BAY
RADBUOY
COWPET BAY
NAZARETH
BENNER BAY
MUSGRAVE LANDING BAY
LONG BAY
ST. THOMAS
CHARLOTTE AMALIE
MORENS BAY
OUTER BRASS
INNER BRASS
LIZARD ROCKS
PRESERRANCE BAY
LINDBERGH BAY
WATER ISLAND
SABA ISLAND

32

Charlotte Amalie, St. Thomas

Great Bay & Cowpet Bay St. Thomas

Christiansted, St. Croix

ROUTE CHARTS

I have drawn these route charts to show the usual routes travelled by yachts and commercial vessels in and around the Virgin Islands. It is well to remember that all anchorages shown on these charts are not necessarily safe overnight anchorages. It is wise, therefore, to check the text as well as the larger scale charts for greater detail in both conditions and soundings when choosing an anchorage.

These route charts are self-explanatory. You may become confused, however, when you find as many as two or three possible route choices to a particular destination. The favoured routes are naturally those which lead through the most protected waters. For instance the preferred route from the main harbour in St. Thomas to Road Harbour, Tortola, under normal conditions would be along the south coast of St. Thomas, through Current Cut, thence along the west coast of St. John leaving Johnson's Reef to port, through Fungi Passage (between Whistling Cay and Mary's Point, St. John), thence on through The Narrows and up the south coast of Tortola to Road Harbour. You may, if you wish, go up the south coast of St. John when making this trip, but the going is very likely to be more rugged because of the open water and the prevailing winds booming out of the east. If you want to cruise the south coast of St. John, you will find it usually much more enjoyable on a broad reach or a run from east to west. Of course, if the wind happens to be blowing well out of the north, which it sometimes does during the winter, cruising along the south coast of St. John can be quite comfortable in either direction.

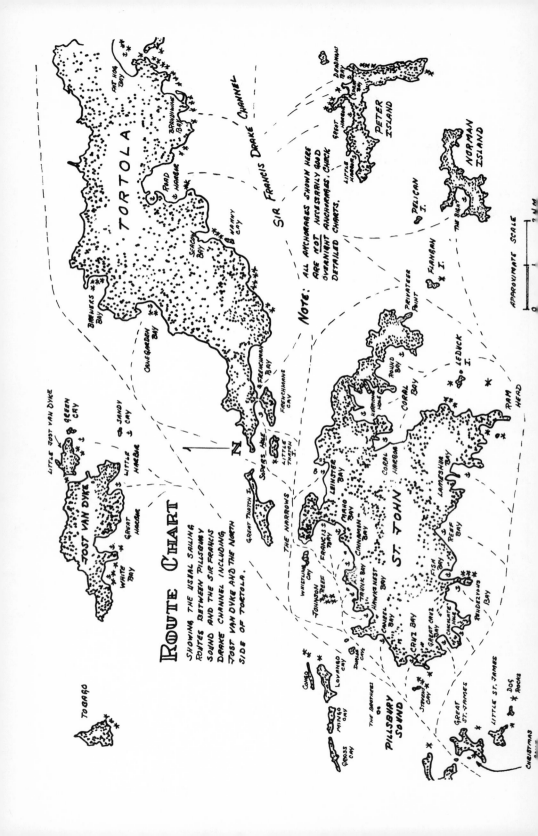

Route Chart

SHOWING THE USUAL SAILING
ROUTES BETWEEN PILLSBURY
SOUND AND THE SIR FRANCIS
DRAKE CHANNEL INCLUDING
JOST VAN DYKE AND THE NORTH
SIDE OF TORTOLA.

NOTE: ALL ANCHORAGES SHOWN HERE
ARE NOT NECESSARILY GOOD
OVERNIGHT ANCHORAGES. CHECK
DETAILED CHARTS.

TORTOLA

SIR FRANCIS DRAKE CHANNEL

FAT HOG BAY

BRANDYWINE BAY

ROAD HARBOUR

SEACOW BAY

NANNY CAY

BREWERS BAY

CANE GARDEN BAY

FRENCHMANS BAY

FRENCHMANS CAY

PETER ISLAND

BRADINNINA BAY

GREAT HARBOUR

LITTLE HARBOUR

LITTLE HARBOUR

NORMAN ISLAND

PELICAN I.

THE BIGHT

PRIVATEER POINT

FLANNAN I.

LEDUCK I.

RAM HEAD

LITTLE JOST VAN DYKE

GREEN CAY

SANDY CAY

JOST VAN DYKE

WHITE BAY

GREAT HARBOUR

LITTLE HARBOUR

N

GREAT THATCH IS.

SOPERS HOLE

LITTLE THATCH

THE NARROWS

PRIVATEER

COIL BAY

CORAL BAY

CORAL HARBOUR

HAULOVER BAY

HAULOVER HAULOVER

LEINSTER BAY

MARY'S BAY

CINNAMON BAY

MAHO BAY

TRUNK BAY

HAWKSNEST BAY

FRANCIS BAY

ST. JOHN

LAMESHUR BAY

REEF BAY

FISH BAY

RENDEZVOUS BAY

GREAT CRUZ BAY

CHOCOLATE HOLE

CONTANT BAY

CRUZ BAY

JOHNSON REEF

WHISTLING CAY

TOBAGO

CONGO CAY

LOVANGO CAY

THE BROTHERS OR MINGO CAY

GROSS CAY

DURLOE CAYS

STEVEN CAY

GREAT ST. JAMES

LITTLE ST. JAMES

DOG ROCKS

PILLSBURY SOUND

CHRISTMAS

APPROXIMATE SCALE

0   1   2 N.M.

The north shore of both St. Thomas and Tortola are generally uninteresting to the yachtsman. These coasts offer little protection and can become extremely uncomfortable during the winter months when either the wind is blowing strongly north of east or the Rollers are coming in. During the summer months when the sea conditions are usually easier these coasts can offer pleasant cruising, though safe overnight anchorages are few and far between. In fact the only anchorage on the north coast that I can recommend as a safe over-night anchorage is Magens Bay on the north coast of St. Thomas; and this anchorage can ONLY be recommended for summer months because the Rollers can make the bay untenable during the winter.

The most protected waters and therefore the most popular areas for cruising in the Virgin Islands are Pillsbury Sound and Sir Francis Drake Channel. In these two bodies of water you will find a good over-night anchorage usually not more than 20 minutes away from almost any given position.

Sketch by Jean Chapman

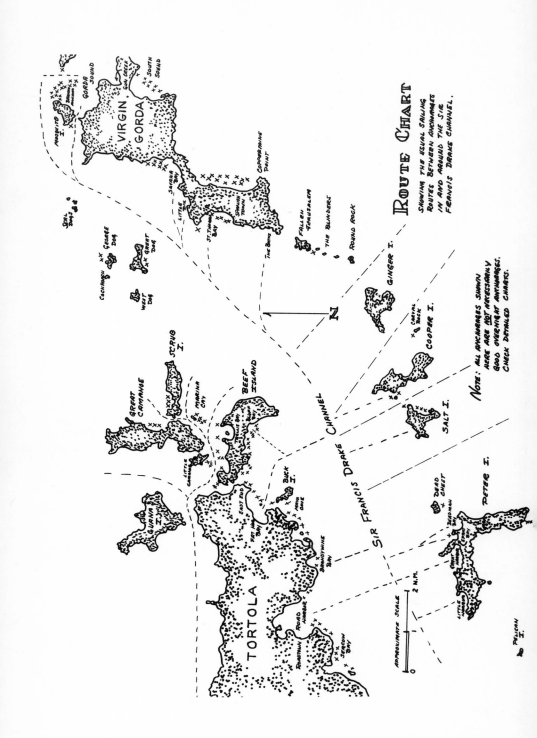

Route Chart

Showing the usual sailing routes between anchorages in and around the Sir Francis Drake Channel.

NOTE: ALL ANCHORAGES SHOWN HERE ARE NOT NECESSARILY GOOD OVERNIGHT ANCHORAGES. CHECK DETAILED CHARTS.

VIRGIN GORDA

GORDA SOUND

SOUTH SOUND

COPPERMINE POINT

SAVANA BAY

LITTLE BAY

ST. THOMAS BAY

SPANISH TOWN

THE BATHS

MOSQUITO I.

SEAL DOGS

CACTUS I.

GEORGE DOG

GREAT DOG

WEST DOG

FALLEN JERUSALEM

THE BLINDERS

ROUND ROCK

GINGER I.

GORAL ROCK

COOPER I.

SALT I.

SCRUB I.

GREAT CAMANOE

MARINA CAY

BEEF ISLAND

LITTLE CAMANOE

GUANA ISLAND

BUCK I.

EAST END

FAT HOG BAY

BRANDYWINE BAY

TORTOLA

ROADTOWN

ROAD HARBOUR

SEACOW BAY

SIR FRANCIS DRAKE CHANNEL

DEAD CHEST

DEADMAN

PETER I.

LITTLE HARBOUR

PELICAN I.

N

APPROXIMATE SCALE   2 N.M.

0

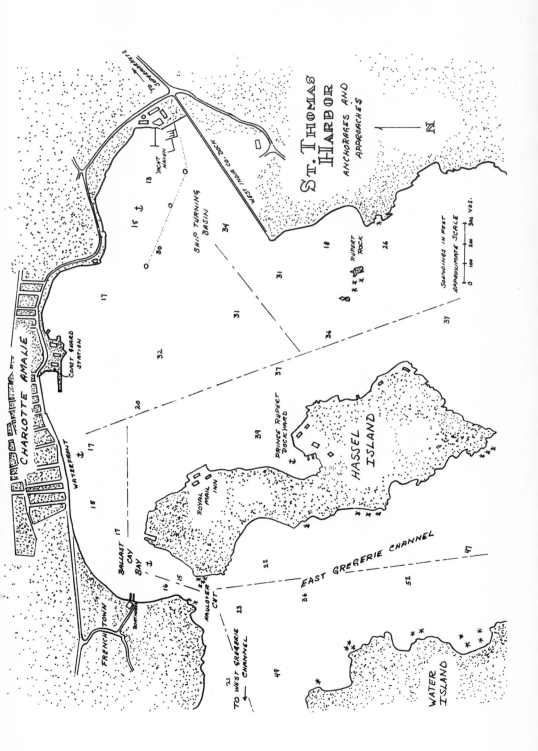

39

ST. THOMAS

ST. THOMAS HARBOR:

There are actually two entrances to St. Thomas Harbor: the **main entrance** which lies between Hassel Island and the eastern side of the harbour and **Haulover Cut** which is the smaller of the two, being a man-made passage between the northwestern tip of Hassel Island and the western corner of the harbour. Yachts drawing less than 10 feet can safely pass through Haulover Cut, while the main harbour entrance is deep enough to accommodate cruise ships.

The approach to the main entrance is open and clear of dangers though care must be taken to stay outside of the Triangle Reef which lies to the southeast of the entrance and is marked by a light buoy. The entrance itself is deep and wide and well marked with proper channel buoys. Yachts may safely pass on either side of Rupert Rock, though no attempt must be made to pass between the Rock and the light buoy which lies several hundred feet to the northwest of the Rock, as there is a reef extending between the two.

There are two approaches to Haulover Cut: the East Gregerie Channel and the West Gregerie Channel. The East Gregerie Channel between Hassel Island and Water Island is deep and free of hazards. The West Gregerie Channel between Water Island and the mainland is also deep and hazard free except for a patch of coral heads which extend from Sandy Point (on the N.W. corner of Water Island) to Sandy Point light buoy which lies approximately 800 feet to the n.w. of the point. These coral heads for the most part are below the surface of the water and are difficult to see. It is therefore important to be sure that you pass the Sandy Point light buoy to the westward. When passing through Haulover Cut stay in mid-channel. You will notice a reef extending from each side of the cut. At one time this reef stretched across the entire entrance with a marsh area behind it which connected Hassel Island to the mainland. In 1937 the government decided to dredge the Cut thus allowing better circulation for the water in the harbour.

LONG BAY

St. Thomas Harbour is the largest commercial harbour in the Virgin Islands and contains no less than 4 anchorage areas that can be used by yachtsmen. The major one of these is Long Bay which is actually the easternmost part of the main harbour. This is presently the most congested anchorage in the Virgin Islands. The charter fleet headquarters here along with a colorful assortment of private yachts, derelicts, etc. When anchoring consideration should be given to the numerous private moorings which infest the area. You must also be careful to anchor well clear of the turning basin and dockage area (marked by large can buoys) which is used by cruise ships and freighters. Yacht Haven is located at the head of this bay and offers fuel, water, showers of sorts, and limited dockage to visiting yachtsmen. The anchorage itself has good holding in mud and the sea conditions are generally calm with a slight trace of a ground sea. Because of the high aspect of the mountains which surround this harbour, the wind can be changeable, so it is a good idea to anchor carefully. Good protection under almost all conditions.

THE WATERFRONT

The area known as **THE WATERFRONT** is the bulkheaded area running along the front of the town on the northern side of the harbour. Here commercial boats tie up and a few private yachts anchor stern-to. This is the least protected of the four anchorages in St. Thomas Harbour and certainly the least comfortable. In fact when a heavy ground sea works in through the main harbour entrance this anchorage can become untenable. It is, however, a convenient spot when taking on supplies in the town or "entering" through U.S. Customs and Immigration. Actually Customs and Immigration prefer that yachts anchor here when entering. Holding is good in a mud bottom.

BALLAST CAY BAY is located in the western corner of the harbor just north of Haulover Cut between Frenchtown and Hassel Island. In the days of sailing ships a cay in this bay was used as a dumping point for ballast prior to loading cargo. There is good protection here for a limited number of yachts. Care must be taken when anchoring to keep the channel clear, because a great deal of commercial traffic moves through the cut. The Boathouse is located on the Frenchtown side with limited facilities for visiting yachtsmen. Holding is good in mud and the seas are generally calm with a light chop except when the commercial traffic goes by.

PRINCE RUPERTS DOCK YARD is located on the eastern side of Hassel Island just inside the main harbour entrance. This is a limited anchorage which can only accommodate a few yachts. There is dock space which is sometimes available and a small anchoring basin. Holding is good in mud and the sea conditions are generally calm except when a ground sea works in through the main harbour entrance.

Swimming is not recommended in any part of St. Thomas Harbour because of the contamination of the water due to sewerage, garbage, etc.

HONEYMOON BAY is located on the western side of Water Island just at the entrance of the West Gregerie Channel. This is a lovely quiet little anchorage which seldom has more than three or four yachts anchored at any one time. There is a sand beach at the head of the Bay which is used by residents of the island as well as guests of the Water Island Hotel. This hotel, located on the southern bluff overlooking the bay, is one of the largest hotels in the Virgin Islands. It has its own ferry service running between the island and the mainland which visiting yachtsmen are welcome to use for a small fee. The ferry lands at the docks in Krum Bay where taxis can usually be found for the trip into town. Meals and rooms may be had at the hotel by prior reservation. For those interested in snorkeling there is a wreck of an old iron steamship lying in about 10 feet of water just off the southern tip of the harbour. When entering stay more or less in the center of the Bay and continue toward the beach. The usual anchorage area is about 50 yards off the beach in about 20 feet of water. Holding is excellent in sand with some grass. The sea conditions are usually calm with good protection when the wind is out of the eastern quadrants. Sometimes a slight ground sea is experienced.

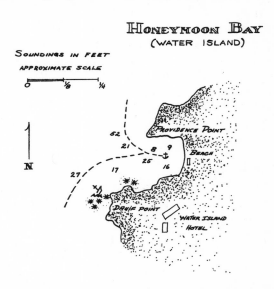

HONEYMOON BAY
(WATER ISLAND)

SOUNDINGS IN FEET
APPROXIMATE SCALE

COWPET BAY is located on the eastern end of the island just south of Current Cut. It is easily recognizable by the half dozen or so private homes which spread across Deck Point to the south of the entrance and the rather awe-inspiring condominium development which is going on at the head of the bay. The Yacht Club of St. Thomas is located here and on weekends the area teems with small class boats sailing briskly about. There are three lines of moorings that have been laid by the yacht club and are rented to club members. The use of moorings by visiting yachtsmen from other recognized clubs can usually be arranged by contacting the house committee chairman. John Fredricks, the club steward, lives on the property and can be very helpful in supplying additional information. There are two beaches in this bay: one immediately in front of the yacht club and the other just to the north. The swimming is good, though the water is not always clear due to the influence of the current which runs through the cut. The effects of this current are also primarily responsible for the rather uncomfortable ground sea condition which prevails throughout most of the year. When the wind is blowing well north of east, however, a very comfortable anchorage can be found in either of the two indentations along the northern side of the bay. Holding is good in deep sand. This is a safe, though not always comfortable, overnight anchorage under almost all conditions.

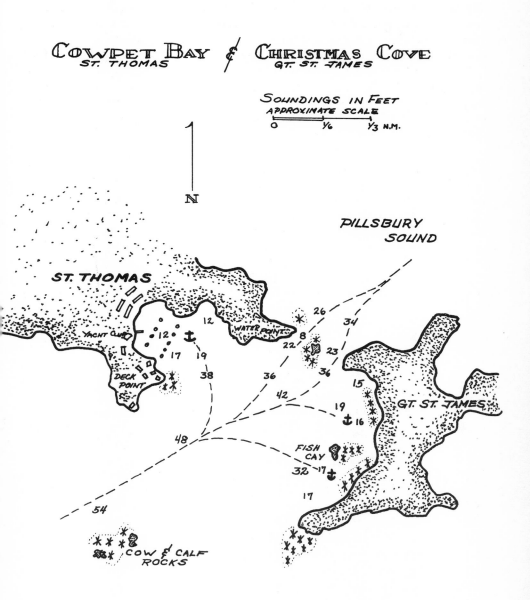

COWPET BAY & CHRISTMAS COVE
ST. THOMAS   GT. ST. JAMES

SOUNDINGS IN FEET
APPROXIMATE SCALE

0   1/6   1/3 N.M.

N

PILLSBURY
SOUND

ST. THOMAS

26
34

12
WATER POINT
8

YACHT CLUB   12   12   23

17   19   36

DECK
POINT   38   36

42   15

19   16

48   GT. ST. JAMES

FISH
CAY

54   3.2   17

17

COW & CALF
ROCKS

CHRISTMAS COVE is located on the western side of Great St. James Island just south of Current Cut and immediately opposite Cowpet Bay. A comfortable anchorage may be found either to the north or to the south of Fish Cay. Care must be taken when anchoring because the lay of the boat is sometimes influenced by the wind blowing through the gut in the island. This anchorage is a popular stop for charterboats based in St. Thomas because it is the last or first (depending on which way you are going) secluded anchorage prior to returning to or leaving St. Thomas harbour. Protection is good when the winds are blowing out of the eastern quadrants. Holding is excellent in sand. The swimming is superb. The approach to either anchorage north or south of Fish Cay is open and clear of dangers. Be careful, however of the reef shoal area which extends to the east and slightly to the north of Fish Cay.

CURRENT CUT The passage between St. Thomas and Great St. James Island, derives its name from the strong current caused by tidal streams which continually run through the cut. The direction of the current naturally depends on the tide. It is, however, usually easy enough to determine the direction of the current when approaching the Cut by careful examination of the rip which is almost always present. The side of the Cut which shows the smooth water is the side from which the current is coming because the "rip" is formed after the current has passed through the Cut. If you see no "rip" the tide is slack and there will be little or no current in the Cut.

Photo by Jay Stone

Current Cut & Pillsbury Sound showing north-bound tidal rip through the cut.

There are two passages through the Cut. The eastern passage, leaving Current Rock to the west, is the one favored by most commercial boats as well as yachts. There is a minimum of 23 feet of water in this passage with ample room for two boats to pass. If you plan to sail through this passage and the wind is blowing from the east or south of east, you can expect to be blanketed by the island just as you are entering the narrowest part of the passage. If the current is running against you, a rather embarrassing situation could arise. Under these conditions it is a good idea to have your auxilliary engine (if you have one) ready for immediate use.

The western passage, leaving Current Rock to the east, is neither as wide nor as deep as the eastern one. Yachts drawing up to 6 feet may pass comfortably through this channel which has a depth of 8 feet at its shallowest point. Care must be taken, however, to stay in mid-channel as there are reefs and rocks on both sides. The current is less on this side of Current Rock and there is little or no blanketing effect from Great St. James Island.

PILLSBURY SOUND: Sailing in this area is generally clear and free of dangers except for the following spots which require careful attention:

When in the vicinity of CABRITA POINT, the headland between Great Bay and Red Hook on St. Thomas, be careful to stand well clear of the rocks just below the surface that extend out into the Sound from the point. It is wise to stay at least 100 yards off this point when passing. These rocks are practically impossible to see until you are on top of them, then they seem to "jump" right up from the bottom. For this reason the outer most rock of this group is locally known as "Jumping Rock". Beware ! ! !

The only other unmarked danger in Pillsbury Sound which could possibly cause trouble is the reef that extends to the southwest from MORAVIAN POINT on St. John. There is a passage through this reef which should only be attempted with extreme caution by yachts drawing less than 9 feet. The recommended route is around the outside of the reef which can be easily negotiated as the outermost part of the reef is awash or breaking in all weather.

All other dangers in Pillsbury Sound are clearly marked or easily distinguished. You may pass inside of SHARK ISLAND off the northeastern coast of St. Thomas if you wish. The Sapphire Bay Beach Club is located here and can be a fun lunch stop. THE BROTHERS are clearly marked and can be left close at hand. There are no hazards to be found when sailing around the DURLOE CAYS except for the obvious sand banks which extend out from shore. The water is so clear that any rocks can easily be seen. It can be beneficial to remember when cruising in this area that the tide running through the Durloe Channel (the passage between the Durloe Cays and St. John) can be quite a bit stronger than the same tide running through the Windward Passage (the passage between the Durloe Cays and Lovango Cay).

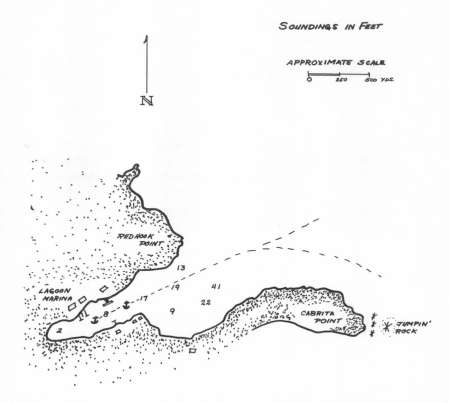

REDHOOK is located just north of Cabrita Point on the eastern end of the island. This is the second busiest harbor in St. Thomas. Ferry boats running between St. Thomas and St. John use the Government Dock on the north side of the harbor, while the Caneel Bay ferry boats and the Park Department boats have their own dock on the south side. The Lagoon Marina is located next to the Government Dock and offers full marina service. Johnny Harms, owner, is probably the best known and best liked fisherman in the Virgin Islands. His marina is considered the headquarters for sport fishing in the islands. Taxis can usually be found around the Government Dock for trips to town or to the supermarket at Ft. Milner. Holding is excellent in soft mud and sand. The bottom shallows to 3 to 4 feet at the head of the bay just west of the Lagoon Marina docks. Though protection is fair to good, there is usually a ground sea or chop, or both, running into the harbor which can make living aboard rather uncomfortable. Swimming is not recommended because the water is generally murky. This is a good anchorage to remember if you are in the area and have to get into town in a hurry or want to pick up passengers without going all the way back to St. Thomas Harbor.

MAGANS BAY, on the north side of St. Thomas, has one of the loveliest beaches on the island. The approach is straight forward and free of dangers, allowing a direct passage to the head of the Bay. The best anchorage is about 100 yards from the beach in the eastern corner. Holding is good in sand. A slight ground sea is generally experienced throughout most of the year. Protection is good under almost all conditions except for the winter when the Rollers can make the anchorage untenable. It is therefore not recommended as an overnight anchorage during the months of October through May. There is a restaurant of sorts on the beach where hamburgers, beer, etc. can be purchased during the day.

ST. JOHN

CRUZ BAY, which is on the western side of St. John just east of Stevens Cay, is the major harbor on the island. Ferry boats from St. Thomas dock here as well as most other commercial traffic. The town surrounding the Bay is usually quiet (except on Friday and Saturday nights) and only limited supplies can be purchased here. The administrator's home and office are located on the headland in the center of the harbor. The U.S. Customs and Immigration office is right across the street from the town jetty. Taxis are usually available at the head of the jetty for tours around this very lovely island. Cruz Bay is the largest town on the island and, besides the limited shopping, can boast of telephone service and even a small hospital. The airboat service connecting St. John to St. Croix also lands here. The approach to Cruz Bay is obstructed in part by a reef which extends to the north from Galge Point. A lighted marker identifies the northernmost edge of this reef. Pass to the north of this marker favoring the northern side of the entrance. Once inside a safe anchorage may be found either

Photo by Jay Stone   **Cruz Bay, St. John**

about 50 yards off the end of the town jetty or in the northern part of the Bay. Holding in both spots is good in a sand bottom. Be wary of the southern part of the Bay as the bottom shoals rapidly in that direction. The jetty itself is used by all commercial vessels entering the harbor so it cannot be recommended for yachtsmen's use. Protection is good and except for the seas created by the commercial traffic the anchorage is calm. Swimming is good.

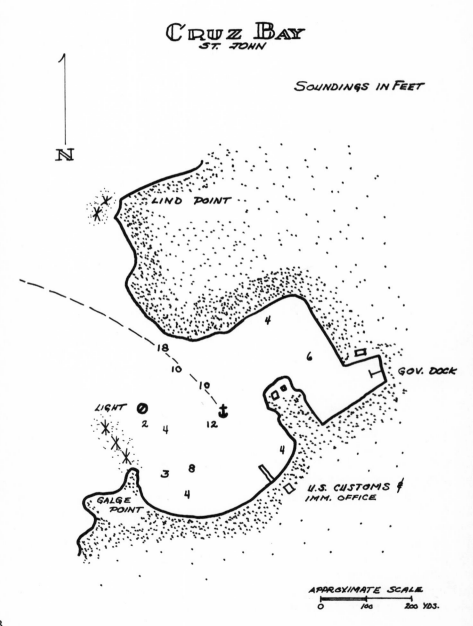

CRUZ BAY
ST. JOHN

SOUNDINGS IN FEET

N

LIND POINT

18

10

10

4

6

GOV. DOCK

LIGHT

2   4   12

3   8

4

4

GALGE
POINT

U.S. CUSTOMS &
IMM. OFFICE

APPROXIMATE SCALE

0   100   200 YDS.

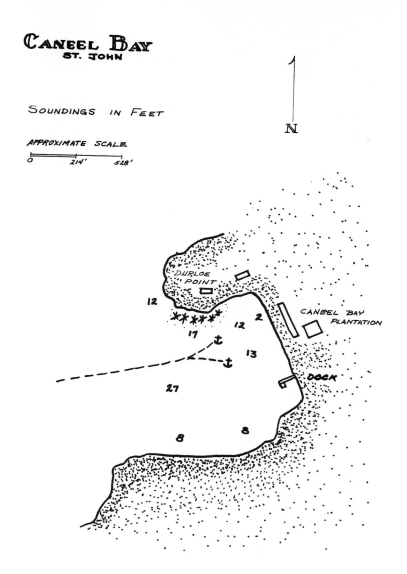

CANEEL BAY
ST. JOHN

SOUNDINGS IN FEET

APPROXIMATE SCALE

0   214'   528'

N

DURLOE
POINT

CANEEL BAY
PLANTATION

DOCK

12

12   2

17

13

27

8   8

CANEEL BAY, also on the western side of the island, lies 3/4 of a mile to the north of Cruz Bay. This is the home of the Caneel Bay Plantation, one of the lovliest and best hotels in the Virgin Islands. Meals may be obtained here by prior reservation. Rooms are available for those wishing to stay ashore, but reservations made well in advance are usually necessary. The approach is open and clear of dangers. The best anchorage is in the northeastern section of the bay, outside of the swimming buoys. Holding is good in sand and the swimming is excellent. There is a pleasant little reef on the northern side of the bay for snorkeling. Though this anchorage offers excellent protection when the wind blows normally out of the eastern quadrants, it can become quite uncomfortable, and even untenable, if the wind moves west of north or if the Rollers come in.

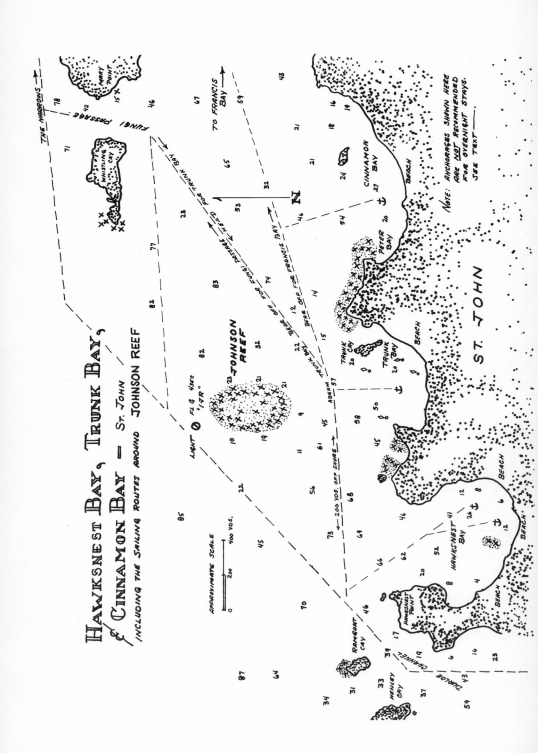

HAWKSNEST BAY, TRUNK BAY, & CINNAMON BAY — ST. JOHN

INCLUDING THE SAILING ROUTES AROUND JOHNSON REEF

N

ST. JOHN

JOHNSON REEF

LIGHT ○ FL.G 4 SEC. "FR"

NOTE: ANCHORAGES SHOWN HERE ARE *NOT* RECOMMENDED FOR OVERNIGHT STAYS. SEE TEXT.

MARY POINT

WHISTLING CAY

THE NARROWS →

FUNGI PASSAGE

TO FRANCIS BAY →

FRANCIS BAY

BEAR OFF HERE FOR TRUNK BAY
BEAR OFF HERE FOR FUNGI PASSAGE HEAD
BEAR OFF HERE FOR FRANCIS BAY

ABEAM TRUNK BAY

← 200 YDS. OFF SHORE →

CINNAMON BAY

BEACH

PETER BAY

TRUNK BAY

TRUNK CAY

BEACH

HAWKSNEST BAY

HAWKSNEST POINT

BEACH

DURLOE CHANNEL

RINGGOLT CAY

HENLEY CAY

APPROXIMATE SCALE
0   200   400 YDS.

HAWKSNEST (HOGSNEST) BAY, located just north and to the east of Caneel Bay, can boast of three separate, lovely beaches. Unfortunately this bay is open to the north and cannot therefore be recommended as an overnight anchorage during the winter months. It can, however, be a pleasant lunch or afternoon stop if conditions permit. The center (southern-most) beach is equipped with barbecue pits, tables, etc. for beach cook-outs. The best anchorage in the bay seems to be in the southeastern corner off one of the two beaches in that area. Enter with caution and stay well clear of the reef in the southern part of the bay. Anchor about 50 to 100 yards off shore. Holding is good in sand and the swimming is excellent. Unfortunately the sea conditions are usually unsettled with a continuous ground sea caused primarily by the strong tidal stream running by the entrance.

TRUNK BAY, just to the east of Hawksnest Bay on the north side of the island; is probably the most popular (and populated) swimming and snorkeling spot east of St. Thomas. Under the supervision of the Park Department, this bay has a marked underwater trail which will appeal to the amateur snorkeler. There is a lunch counter on the beach where sandwiches and drinks may be purchased. The approach is simple enough: the Park Department maintains four buoys just off the beach. You are expected to anchor between these. A ranger or beach supervisor will usually paddle out and direct you to a preferred anchorage. Holding is good in sand and the swimming is excellent. The sea conditions are usually favorable for a lunch or swim stop, though a slight ground sea is almost always in evidence. Unfortunately this is another anchorage which cannot be recommended for overnight stays during the winter months as the Rollers can make the area quite untenable.

CINNAMON BAY, lies just east of Trunk Bay on the north shore of the island. This bay also has a lovely beach which is under the supervision of the Park Department. There are camping facilities, barbecues, toilets, etc. for those wishing to camp out in the unspoiled beauty of the park. Rental cabins are also available near the beach. For those wishing to stay ashore reservations should be made well in advance through the Park Department (see index). The anchorage is usually comfortable enough under standard conditions with just a hint of a ground sea. Because of it's exposure to the north, however, this is not a recommended overnight anchorage during the winter months. Holding is good in sand and the swimming is excellent.

MAHO BAY, the small area in the southeast corner of Francis Bay can be a lovely overnight anchorage during the summer months. In the winter, however, an uncomfortable ground sea can be experienced. The approach is open and clear of dangers and a good anchorage may be found within 50-100 yards of the beach. Holding is good in sand and grass. Swimming is excellent. The house on the bluff above the bay belongs to Mrs. Ethel McCully, a great gal on the sunny side of 80, who built the house with 6

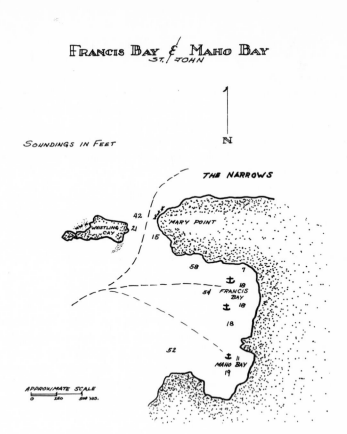

donkeys, a couple of natives and her own two hands. She wrote a very amusing book about it which she originally titled "I Did It With Donkeys". The publisher said "no" to this title, however, so she changed it to "Grandma Raises The Roof".

JOHNSON REEF

JOHNSON REEF, lying just to the north of Trunk Bay off the northwestern side of St. John, is a navigation hazard which should receive careful attention. There is deep water running completely around this reef where yachts may pass in complete safety. The western side of the reef bordering the Windward Passage is steep-to and can be left close at hand. The eastern side of the reef, however, shoals rather slowly in spots with isolated outcroppings and should be approached with caution. For those wishing to pass to the south of the reef from west to east it is a good idea to stay within 200 yards of the general coastline of St. John until abeam Trunk Bay. You may then consider yourself clear of the hazard and continue your course either directly to Fungi Passage or on into Francis Bay. If approaching from the Fungi Passage, set your course to the center or western end of Trunk Bay and carry on until abeam the Bay and not more than 200 yards off the general coastline of St. John. You may then continue your course to the westward keeping approximately 200 yards offshore until the Johnson Reef light buoy bears 10 degrees or better. At this time you may consider yourself clear of the hazard.

This reef breaks in anything but the calmest seas, and when the rollers are coming in the seas have been known to break all the way from the reef to the headland on St. John. Under these conditions it is generally a good idea to pass to the north of the reef. When passing to the north in either direction, simply establish and maintain a course to the north of an east-west line extending eastward from the Johnson Reef light buoy until well clear of the hazard.

This reef can prove interesting for the skindiver and snorkeler when sea conditions are calm. Lobster can usually be found in relatively shallow water along the eastern side of the reef. It is well to remember, however, that this reef is under the supervision of the Park Department, so abide by their rules (see: Virgin Islands National Park) while in the area.

FUNGI PASSAGE

FUNGI PASSAGE, located between Whistling Cay and Mary Point, St.John, is a deep passage to both sides with very little current activity ever experienced. The only possible danger when approaching this passage is a shoal area which extends a short way to the south from the south-eastern tip of Whistling Cay. As you pass through the Cut you will see the ruin of an old customs house on the eastern shore of the Cay. This ruin was directly in line-of-sight of another customs house located on either Little Thatch or Frenchmans Cay on the north side of The Narrows. Apparently these two customs houses were situated in this manner to enable signals to be passed back and forth. The north side of the passage is also historically interesting. Mary Point is the spot where hundreds of slaves jumped to their death rather than submit to capture after the great slave uprising in 1733.

THE NARROWS

Both current and wind funnel through this passage, but the seas seldom exceed 2 to 3 feet. The area is free of hazards and yachts may sail comfortably to within 50 yards of either shore. A prevailing tidal stream makes the St. John side preferable for eastbound passages and the Tortola side for westbound (see "Tidal Streams").

ST. JOHN (cont.)

FRANCIS BAY is located on the north shore of the island just south and to the east of Fungi Passage. It is a comfortable anchorage under almost all conditions. The approach offers no problem. You may anchor within 50 to 100 yards of the beach. This beach is a haven for local fishermen who dry their nets here and draw their boats up onto the sand. Holding is good in sandy-mud and grass. Swimming is excellent. I have had a great deal of fun at night here shining a flashlight over the side of the boat. When the water is clear the beam of light extends like a column straight to the bottom. When held still this column of light will attract a variety of fish. Some attack it; others just come for a look; all are interested and interesting to watch. If you look closely you might see a small sand shark circling quietly just outside the perimeter of light.

LEINSTER BAY is on the northern side of the island just across The Narrows from Little Thatch Island. There are three anchorages in this Bay, all of which are safe in any but the most adverse conditions. The approach to the Bay between Waterlemon Cay and the western headland is clear of dangers. Yachts may also pass to the east of Waterlemon Cay through a narrow channel which has 12 feet of water at it's shallowest point, but extreme caution is recommended. The two most popular anchorages in this Bay are on the eastern side. The one I like best is just to the south of Waterlemon Cay where an anchor may be dropped in 20 feet of water no more than 50 feet off a very tiny sandy beach on the southeastern end of the Cay. This anchorage offers little protection from the trade winds (which is great when it's buggy) but the seas are always calm because of the excellent protection afforded by the Cay and the eastern headland of the Bay. Holding is excellent in sand, but there is only room for a limited number of yachts as the bottom drops off quite rapidly. Swimming and snorkeling are excellent with interesting exploration around the entire Cay. This is one of my favorite spots.

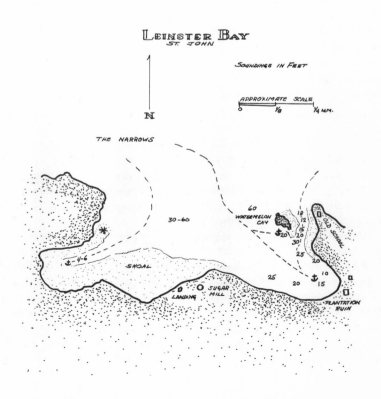

LEINSTER BAY
ST. JOHN

Photo by Jay Stone

Limejuice Bay, St. John

The other (and larger) anchorage in the eastern part of the Bay is in Waterlemon Bay (or Limejuice Bay) which lies in the extreme southeast corner of Leinster Bay. Again, there are no hazards in this small bay. The water remains 20 to 25 feet deep within 50 to 100 feet of the entire shore line. As you approach the very head of the bay, however, the water does shoal a slight bit close to the shore. Holding is good in sand and grass and the sea conditions are calm. Swimming is good.

There is an old plantation ruin lying at the head of the bay which was once known as Limetree Plantation. This is an interesting ruin to explore though I understand that someone bought the property and is planning to restore it. From this plantation a trail leads to the reform school which sits on the northeasternmost point of Leinster Bay. This building was originally a Masonic Lodge . . . the first one built in the Western Hemisphere! ! !

The third and least often used anchorage in Leinster Bay is Mary Creek located in the very westernmost part of the Bay. There is a sand bank across the entrance to this anchorage which limits draft to 4 feet or less. Once over the bar, however, the Creek widens and deepens to approximately 6 feet. Holding is excellent in sand. The sea conditions are always calm even though the anchorage is off a lee shore. Advantageously this windward position results in a relatively bug-free anchorage during the damp seasons. There is room here for two or three yachts to anchor comfortably.

55

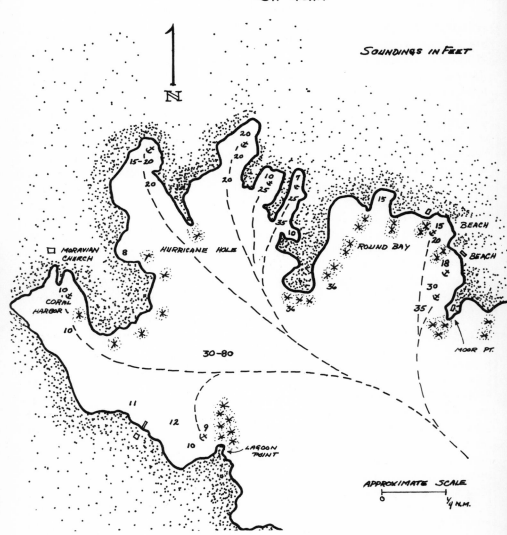

CORAL BAY
ST. JOHN

SOUNDINGS IN FEET

N

15-20
20
15-20
20
20
20
20

10
25

7
25

35
10
15

□ MORAVIAN
CHURCH

HURRICANE HOLE

ROUND BAY

BEACH
15
20
18
30
35
BEACH

8

10
CORAL
HARBOR

36

36

MOOR PT.

10

30-80

11
12
9
10
LAGOON
POINT

APPROXIMATE SCALE

0   ¼ N.M.

On sailing into Leinster Bay you will notice some ruins on the southern slope overlooking the Bay. This is the former Annaberg Plantation which was one of the largest sugar manufacturing plantations on the island. These ruins, maintained by the Park Department, are well worth the visit. On the path leading to the sugar mill you will find a small stand which usually contains pamphlets describing the ruins. There is a dock to the west of the ruins where a dinghy may be taken in, or you can walk along the road from Limetree Plantation.

HAULOVER BAY, just 2½ miles east of Leinster Bay, is the only other anchorage on the north coast of St. John which holds any interest for visiting yachtsmen. It derives it's name from the lowland at the head of the Bay. During times gone by fishermen hauled their boats over this lowland into Coral Bay rather than sailing or rowing them around the point. The approach to the Bay is open and free of hazards as long as you stay more or less in mid-channel; there being shoals which extend out slightly from both sides of the entrance. The best anchorage is in the southeasternmost corner of the Bay where a small sandy beach is to be found. On approaching this beach you will pass an old, but very solid, tree to starboard which is up-ended in the water. On closer examination you will find that it is securely stuck to the bottom . . . in 40 feet of water! ! ! This tree can serve quite well as a stern anchor or a lunch mooring. The depth of the Bay ranges from 60 to 20 feet, but as you approach to within 10 yards of the beach, the bottom shoals to 10 feet or less. This is a very small anchorage having room for only one or two boats, but the protection is good under almost all conditions. Holding is excellent in soft sand and the sea conditions are usually calm. Swimming is excellent.

CORAL BAY, the largest bay on St. John, is located on the southeastern side of the island. The Bay has numerous anchorages and contains many points of interest for the visiting yachtsman. It is divided into three sections. The easternmost and undoubtedly the most beautiful of these is **ROUND BAY.** There are several lovely beaches located here and anchoring is usually quite pleasant though a slight ground sea is almost always experienced. The approach is simple and straight forward with no hidden dangers. When entering from the east stay well clear of the reef off Moor Point. A good anchorage may be found off any of the beaches on the eastern side. Holding is excellent in sand and the protection is good under almost all conditions. The two little beaches on the north side of Round Bay are rocky and not too interesting, and anchoring off of them can sometimes be rather uncomfortable. The western side of the Bay should be avoided as a rather nasty reef extends the full length of it. This reef is always breaking or awash.

If the ground seas become too uncomfortable in Round Bay, you can move into one of the four small bays in **HURRICANE HOLE,** located just to the west of Round Bay. These bays are extremely well protected and

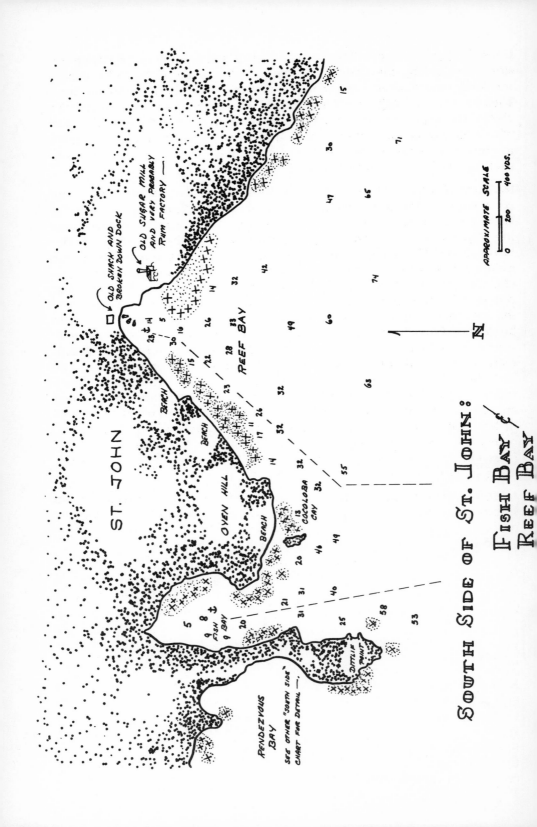

ST. JOHN

OLD SHACK AND
BROKEN DOWN DOCK

OLD SUGAR MILL
AND VERY PROBABLY
RUM FACTORY

BEACH

BEACH

BEACH

BEACH

OVEN HILL

COCOLOBA
CAY

FISH
BAY

DITTLIF
POINT

RENDEZVOUS
BAY

SEE OTHER "SOUTH SIDE"
CHART FOR DETAIL

REEF BAY

N

APPROXIMATE SCALE

0   200   400 YDS.

SOUTH SIDE OF ST. JOHN:

FISH BAY &
REEF BAY

holding is excellent in soft sand and mud. There is nothing of interest in these bays except solitude, and the bugs can become quite fierce during the rainy seasons. Because of their protection, the sea conditions in these bays are always calm. Needless to say, this section of Coral Bay becomes one of the major havens for yachtsmen during the hurricane season. The approaches to all four of these bays are deep and free of hidden dangers. The bottom shoals rather rapidly close to shore, but the middle grounds are deep enough to take almost any yacht.

South of Hurricane Hole and slightly to the westward an anchorage can be found in **CORAL HARBOR.** This area is not so deep as the rest of Coral Bay and should therefore be approached with caution. Yachts drawing less than 9 feet can proceed a good distance into the anchorage, but those drawing over 6 feet should stay in mid-channel and proceed with extreme care. There are no hidden dangers in the approach except shallow water and a rock here and there just off the northeastern shore. The deeper draft yachts should favor this shore slightly when entering. The anchorage is well protected under most conditions and holding is good in sand and mud. The sea conditions are generally calm. There is a small native community clustered around the head of the harbor where practically nothing can be obtained . . . except smiles and conversation. The Moravian church, which is easy to spot from the anchorage has a very interesting history. Perhaps you can persuade one of the locals to tell you the story.

There is another anchorage in Coral Bay just off the southern shore to the west of **LAGOON POINT.** This anchorage is well protected by a reef which extends north from the point. Holding is good in sand and the sea conditions are generally calm. If approaching from the east, be sure to stand well clear of the reef. Swimming is excellent here and some good snorkeling can be found on calm days along the outside of the reef.

When approaching Coral Bay from the south, extreme care should be taken to stay well clear of the **Eagle Shoal** which is ½ mile to the east of Ram Head. If passing inside of the Shoal, leave the shore close at hand (about 100 yards off) and continue northward between Sabbat Point and Leduck Island. Once by the island you will be clear of dangers. When passing Eagle Shoal to the east, stay south of Ram Head until the easternmost point of Leduck Island bears less than 359 degrees. Keep this easternmost point of the island bearing less than 359 degrees until well clear of the Shoal.

REEF BAY, on the south side of the island, is an interesting lunch stop and afternoon anchorage, though not recommended for overnight stays unless the wind is well to the north and expected to stay there. A ground sea is experienced most of the time and when the wind is south of east, this condition can prove to be quite uncomfortable. When approaching the anchorage, located in the northwestern corner, stay well clear of the reefs which extend along both sides of the Bay. These reefs are easy to

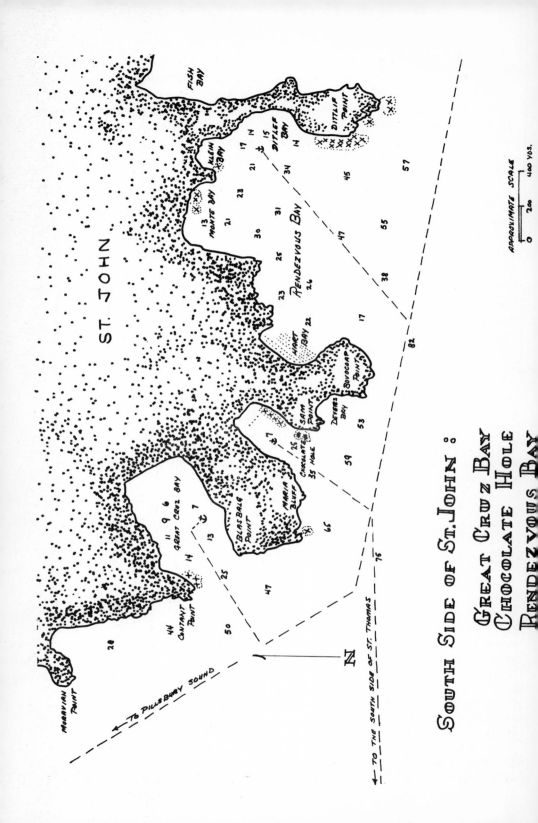

ST. JOHN

FISH BAY

DITTLIF POINT

DITTLIF BAY

KLEIN BAY

MONTE BAY

RENDEZVOUS BAY

HART BAY

SAM POINT

CHOCOLATE HOLE

BOVOCAP POINT

DEVERS BAY

MARIA BLUFF

BLAS BALA POINT

GREAT CRUZ BAY

CONTANT POINT

MORAVIAN POINT

N

← TO PILLSBURY SOUND

← TO THE SOUTH SIDE OF ST. THOMAS

APPROXIMATE SCALE

0   200   400 YDS.

SOUTH SIDE OF ST. JOHN:
GREAT CRUZ BAY
CHOCOLATE HOLE
RENDEZVOUS BAY

distinguish, being either awash or breaking at all times. Out from these reefs to the center of the Bay the water is deep and clear of dangers. On approaching the anchorage you will find the reefs along both sides dwindling to nothing. Continue slowly past the reefs and into the head of the Bay where a shack can be seen on the beach with a broken down dock extending from it. A good anchorage can be found in 7 to 10 feet of water about 200 feet from the end of the dock. If you draw over 6 feet enter this area with extreme caution, following the dark water in. Holding is good in sand, mud and some grass. Just to the west of the anchorage lies an old mill who's stack is visible above the tree tops. The area also abounds with lime trees. Once ashore you might decide to follow the path which leads to a waterfall (during the rainy season) and some old indian petroglyphs. Since this path crosses private property, it is important to obtain permission from the landowner. A bottle of gin and a polite, persuasive manner will go a long way here. Swimming and snorkeling are both excellent in this anchorage.

FISH BAY, just to the west of Reef Bay on the south side of St. John, is a good anchorage under all normal conditions though a slight ground sea is almost always experienced. When approaching the anchorage stay in mid-channel as reefs extend a short way from both the eastern and western shores at the entrance. After passing into the Bay proceed with caution as the bottom tends to shoal rather rapidly, Yachts drawing 8 to 10 feet should anchor just outside the mouth of the Bay while those with lesser draft may continue well in. Holding is good in sand and mud, and the sea conditions are generally calm. There is a little beach on the eastern side of the entrance which is surrounded by reef, but sort of fun to explore. Farther to the east, just outside the entrance and behind Cocolba Cay, is another larger beach which can be approached by dinghy when conditions allow. Caution must be taken, however, as there are numerous coral heads along the approach to this beach and the seas can be quite unsettled, even under normal conditions. For those interested in fishing, there are some lovely bonefish flats at the head of the Bay. Swimming is good.

RONDEZVOUS BAY is a large, rather open bay lying just to the west of Fish Bay. It offers little protection for overnight anchoring unless the wind is well north of east. There is, however, one anchorage in this bay which is adequate under normal conditions and almost always a pleasant lunch or afternoon stop. This anchorage is just off the small beach in Ditleff Bay, which is on the eastern side of the main Bay. Holding is good in sand and grass. A slight ground sea is experienced throughout the year. The approach to this anchorage is clear of dangers and swimming is excellent. The remainder of Rondezvous Bay is generally much too unsettled to be considered a comfortable anchorage.

CHOCOLATE HOLE, just west of Rondezvous Bay, is a pleasant, quiet, well protected anchorage. The approach is straight forward, though on entering you should favor the western side as a small reef extends about 15 to 20 yards out from the eastern shore. Yachts drawing 6 feet or less may approach to within 20 yards of the first line of moorings. From this point to the head of the Bay the bottom shoals rapidly to 4 feet or less. Holding is good in sand and grass, and the sea conditions are generally calm. Swimming is good and the little reef on the eastern side of the entrance is interesting for snorkelers. There seems to be quite a bit of construction activity on the slopes surrounding the Bay, so it should not be long before the area is filled with vacation homes, hotels, etc. . . . oh, well.

GREAT CRUZ BAY is just north of Chocolate Hole. Though not particularly scenic, this bay does afford good protection in all but the most adverse conditions. The seas are generally calm, though a slight ground sea is very often in evidence. Holding is good in sand and grass. At the head of the Bay the bottom begins to shoal and should be approached with caution. The entrance is wide and unobstructed except for a small reef which extends from the north side. The best anchorage seems to be about half way to the head of the Bay and 50 yards or so off the southeastern shore.

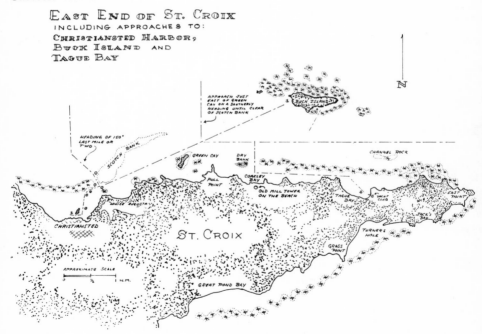

EAST END OF ST. CROIX
INCLUDING APPROACHES TO:
CHRISTIANSTED HARBOR,
BUCK ISLAND AND
TAGUE BAY

ST. CROIX

THE PASSAGE BETWEEN ST. THOMAS AND ST. CROIX. St. Croix is the largest and most industrially oriented of the American Virgin Islands. Lying due south of St. Thomas across a 35 mile expanse of open, and sometimes quite rough, Caribbean Sea which reaches a depth of almost

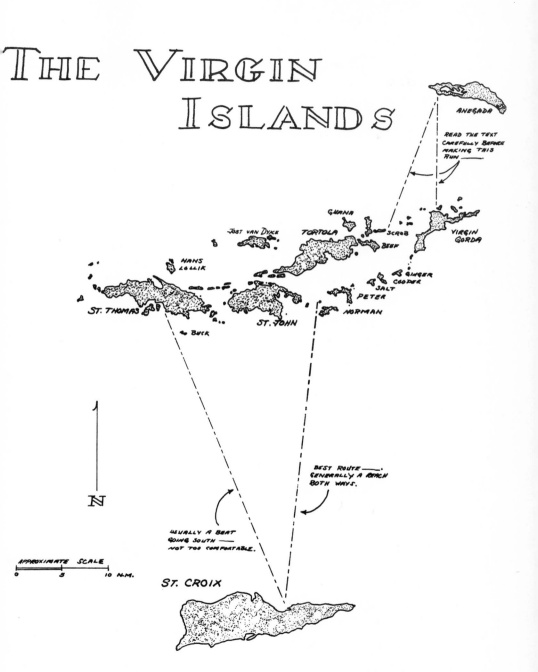

THE VIRGIN ISLANDS

ANEGADA

READ THE TEXT
CAREFULLY BEFORE
MAKING THIS
RUN

GUANA

JOST VAN DYKE   TORTOLA

SCRUB   VIRGIN
GORDA

BEEF

HANS
LOLLIK

GINGER
COOPER

SALT

PETER

ST. THOMAS

ST. JOHN

NORMAN

BUCK

BEST ROUTE —
GENERALLY A REACH
BOTH WAYS.

N

USUALLY A BEAT
GOING SOUTH —
NOT TOO COMFORTABLE.

APPROXIMATE SCALE

0   5   10 N.M.

ST. CROIX

63

CHRISTIANSTED HARBOR
ST. CROIX

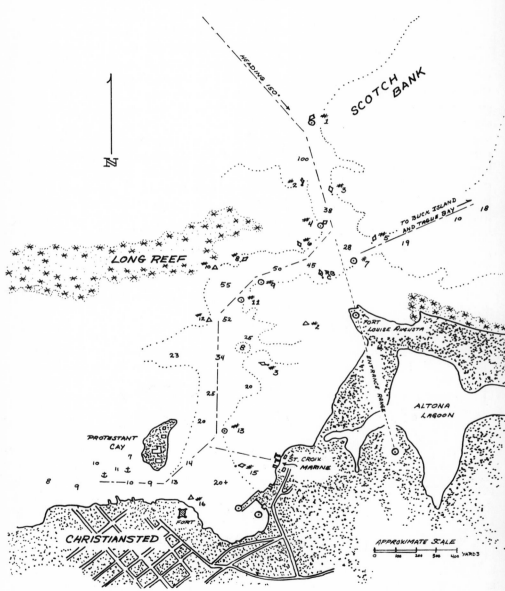

N

HEADING 150°

SCOTCH BANK

100

☒ #1

☒ #2 ☒ #3

38

TO BUCK ISLAND AND TAGUE BAY   18

☒ #4   28   19   10

☒ #6   ☒ #5

LONG REEF   ☒ #8   45   ☒ #7

10△   50   RB C

55   ☒ #9

☒ #11

12△   52

25   △ #2

FORT LOUISE AUGUSTA

23   34   8

☒ #3   ENTRANCE RANGE

25   20   ALTONA LAGOON

20   ☒ #13

PROTESTANT CAY   7   14   ST. CROIX MARINE

10   ☒ #15

8   9   10 — 9 — 13   20+

△ #16

FORT

CHRISTIANSTED

APPROXIMATE SCALE

0   100   200   300   400 YARDS

5 miles in places, St. Croix is not on the usual itinerary of the vacationing yachtsman. However, if you have time to spare and can afford to choose the days of your crossing, the sail both over and back can be a comfortable as well as an exhilarating experience.

In planning your trip to or from St. Croix one of the things which must receive careful consideration, if you are to get maximum comfort and enjoyment out of the cruise, is the direction and strength of the wind. If the wind is blowing from the east or south of east, which it usually does, you should start your **southbound crossing** from the Flanagan or Salt Island Passage. This will allow a close reach, or at least the cracking of sheets, going across and will certainly be more comfortable and faster than the wet beat to weather that most certainly would have been experienced on leaving from the Main Harbor in St. Thomas. Plan to leave no later than 9:00 A.M. and you should have ample time to make your anchorage in St. Croix during daylight hours. The **northbound trip** is usually the easier crossing with a comfortable reach or run all the way. Unfortunately, however, the wind can very often blow out of the north during the winter months which makes the northbound trip a dead beat to weather. At a time like this it is nice to have a few days in hand, so that you can wait for more favorable conditions; though this north wind has been known to continue for weeks at a time. It is also well to remember that a slight westerly current runs between St. Thomas and St. Croix. This current increases and decreases slightly with the strength of the trade winds and is therefore not consistant. Generally speaking, 1½ knots of current for the entire passage is a safe enough estimate for navigation purposes.

CHRISTIANSTED HARBOR. The major harbor as well as the major town on this island is Christiansted, located almost centrally on the north coast. The entrance to Christiansted Harbor, though well marked, can prove confusing to the visiting yachtsman and should be negotiated with caution. On **approaching** the entrance first locate and identify the outermost buoy (no. "1", fl., 2½ sec., white). To be sure of avoiding the Scotch Bank establish a heading of 150 degrees to this buoy while still a mile or two miles at sea. The buoy should be left close to port on a heading which should line you up with Fort Louis Agusta on the point. Maintain this course passing no. "2" red nun to starboard, the no. "3" black can to port, and the no. "4" quick-flashing red light buoy to starboard. You may then begin an easy 90 degree turn to starboard making sure that you keep the no. "6" red nun on the starboard hand. Once abeam the no. "6" red nun start bearing off slightly to port towards the no. "9" flashing green light marker which is a pylon. When abeam this marker you should again bear slightly away to port being sure to keep the no. "11" quick-flashing green light marker (also a pylon) on the port hand. Continue more or less on the same course moving over to the western side of the channel in the direction of the no. "12" red marker post. On approaching this post (approximately 10 yards distant) alter course to a southerly direction, keeping the post on your starboard hand and heading toward the no. "13" flashing white light marker (single post) which must be left to port. This manoeuver is designed to keep you well clear of the Little Middle Ground which is covered by not more than 7 to 8 feet of water and located just to the northwest of the Lagoon Bank black can. Once abeam the no. "13" marker continue around Protestant Cay, leaving it not less than 50 yards to starboard. The yacht anchorage is located off the western side of this Cay. Sea conditions here are generally calm with good holding in sand. The main part of town is just a short dinghy trip to the south and contains a wide variety of shops, restaurants, hotels, etc. . . . . a rather delightful anchorage.

BUCK ISLAND is a lovely spot for a day's outing from Christiansted or even an overnight stay. To sail from the anchorage in Christiansted Harbor to Buck Island simply go out the main channel entrance until abeam the no. "7" light marker. Leave the main channel here and set a course directly for the anchorage on the western end of Buck Island, leaving the no. "5" black can to port and Green Cay at least 50 yards to starboard. In sailing this course you will quite often find the wind directly on the nose because of the prevailing easterly conditions. The seas are generally easy, however, which makes for a very pleasant sail. It is advisable when short-tacking along this course to pay close attention to your position until well clear of the Scotch Bank. This Bank is hard to detect under some conditions, so keep a careful lookout. The best anchorage at Buck Island is just off a lovely sand beach on the western tip of the island. The approach is open and clear of hazards from the southwest and a comfortable anchorage may be found quite close to the beach. Holding is good in sand and the swimming is excellent. The sea conditions are generally easy, making this a pleasant overnight anchorage. The famous Buck Island Underwater Park is located on the eastern end inside of an outer reef which completely surrounds that end of the island. There is an opening in this outer reef on the southeastern side where yachts drawing 5 feet or less can come inside and anchor. Approach this anchorage with caution as there are numerous coral heads scattered about both inside and out. Once inside the holding conditions are good in sand and the best anchorage is close to shore in the northwest corner. A ground sea is generally experienced in this anchorage making it not too comfortable for overnight stays. The Park Department has underwater plaques placed about which describe the sea life found in the area. Remember, this is Park Department property; so no spear guns. (see: Virgin Islands National Park) If you want to do it the easy way, there are excursion boats which leave from Christiansted every day taking eager snorkelers to this reef.

TAGUE BAY, located inside the reef which stretches along the northeastern end of St. Croix, is the home of the St. Croix Yacht Club. During the weekends there is a great deal of activity with racing dinghys going on here. On approaching from the west, establish an easterly heading once

Buck Island Near St. Croix

Photo by Dukane Press, Inc.

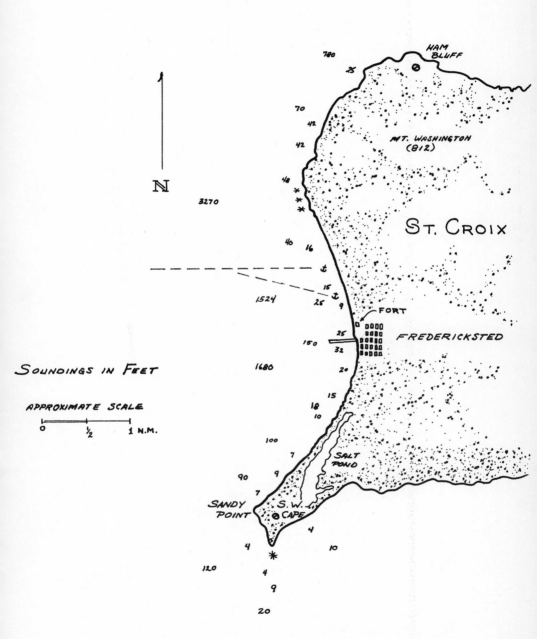

FREDERICKSTED
ST. CROIX

N

SOUNDINGS IN FEET

APPROXIMATE SCALE

0   ½   1 N.M.

HAM BLUFF

MT. WASHINGTON (812)

ST. CROIX

FORT

FREDERICKSTED

SALT POND

SANDY POINT

S.W. CAPE

past Green Cay and maintain this until the old mill tower on the beach at Coakley Bay bears due south. At this time alter course to a heading of south and proceed directly toward the mill tower. Pass through the opening in the reef leaving the sand spit to starboard and the breaking reef to port. The opening is approximately 150 yards wide, but it is a good idea to maintain your position in mid-channel until well clear. There is a minimum of 12 feet of water through the reef and all the way to Tague Bay. Once inside the reef continue straight along to Tague Bay, staying in mid-channel or slightly to the south as occasional coral heads can be encountered close to the reef. All of these heads, incidentally, are clearly visible below the surface, so keep a sharp lookout. Upon reaching the westernmost point of Tague Bay, yachts drawing less than 6 feet may continue straight in to the Yacht Club dock. Those with greater draft can proceed no farther than half the distance because the bottom shoals rapidly once inside the Bay. The southwestern section of the Bay (southwest of a line drawn from the western tip of the Bay to the Yacht Club) is quite shallow and should be avoided. Holding is good in sand and grass, and the sea conditions are always calm. The swimming is excellent.

FREDERICKSTED, located on the western end of St. Croix, is the second largest town on the island. There are ample bars, restaurants, shops, etc. which cater primarily to the cruise ships using the town's large commercial wharf. This anchorage is an open roadsted and can therefore not offer positive protection under any but the standard easterly conditions. The best yacht anchorage is north of the commercial jetty and within 100 yards of shore. Holding is good in sand. The sea conditions are generally easy with a slight ground sea experienced most of the time. Swimming is good. This anchorage is not very popular with yachtsmen because of it's open aspect as well as it's out-of-the-way position. It is, nevertheless, a rather lovely spot.

Sketch by Jean Chapman

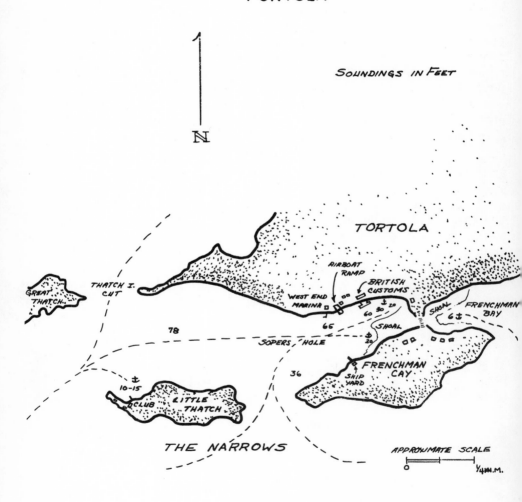

LITTLE THATCH & WEST END
TORTOLA

N

SOUNDINGS IN FEET

TORTOLA

AIRBOAT
RAMP

BRITISH
CUSTOMS

GREAT
THATCH

THATCH I.
CUT

WEST END
MARINA

FRENCHMAN
BAY

SHOAL

6⚓

78

65

60 30
20

SHOAL

SOPERS HOLE

20

FRENCHMAN
CAY

36

⚓
10-15

SHIP
YARD

CLUB

LITTLE
THATCH

THE NARROWS

APPROXIMATE SCALE

0   ¼ N.M.

THE BRITISH VIRGIN ISLANDS

Roadtown, Tortola

Photo by Jay Stone

WICHAMS KEY

TOWN DOCK

THE BRITISH VIRGIN ISLANDS
TORTOLA

During the 18th and 19th centuries the residents of Tortola were quite openly engaged in the business of piracy on the high seas. Apparently businessmen, doctors, and the like—all respected members of their community—owned pirate ships which preyed on shipping throughout the islands. Goods, slaves, produce, etc. were hijacked by these "Tortola Pirates" and either ransomed back to the owners or sold elsewhere. Because of the lack of proper government protection, the grim business flourished for many years; sometimes even with the help of the oppressed side. In fact some historians feel that the "Custom House" on Whistling Cay was also used as a signaling station to alert the pirates of approaching shipping. The descendants of these pirates are still to be found on the island; though my personal opinion is that most of them must have moved to St. Thomas . . .

Tortola is the most populated as well as one of the largest of the British Virgin Islands and is presently experiencing the greatest economic boom in it's history due to the overflowing prosperity from the American Virgin Islands.

WEST END is a small community located in Sopers Hole on the western end of the island. Only meager supplies are available in the town, though the Tortola ferry service from the American Virgins does stop at the Government Dock and the airboat also lands here. Taxis can usually be found at the Dock for trips into town (get a price before you get in). Customs and Immigration officials have their offices on the dock and can usually be found somewhere around the area during normal working hours. The approaches to West End are straight forward with no hidden obstacles. An entrance into Sopers Hole can be made from The Narrows around either side of Little Thatch Island or from the north through the Thatch Island Cut. The best anchorage in this harbor for yachts up to 60 feet is in the northeasternmost corner. The approach is clear of dangers. Continue past the Government Dock on a northeasterly heading towards the tin shed at the head of the bay. An anchorage may be found in 20 feet of water not more than 50 yards off shore. Holding is good in sandy mud and the protection is excellent with generally calm sea conditions. Another good anchorage in this harbor is just off the shoal ledge which runs out from Frenchman's Cay. There is good holding here in a depth of about 20 feet in a sand bottom. The protection is not as good as in the northeastern corner, but it is better than the remainder of the bay, which is also quite deep. There is a small marina of sorts just to the west of the airboat ramp. It is run by a Frenchman, Paul Gouin, who can be surprisingly helpful if you need assistance.

LITTLE THATCH ISLAND has a lovely anchorage off of a beautiful little beach on the northwestern corner of the island. There is an attractive guest house facility here. Meals and rooms are available by reservation (contact them on the "childrens hour" for dinner). An anchorage may be found just outside of the moorings. Holding is good in sand and the swimming is excellent. Unfortunately this anchorage cannot be recommended for overnight stays during the winter months because of the uncomfortable sea conditions so often experienced. Even during the summer months a ground sea almost always prevails, undoubtedly caused by the tidal stream which sweeps through Thatch Cut.

FRENCHMAN BAY has a rather pleasant anchorage just off the northeastern shore of Frenchman Cay. As you round the eastern point of Frenchman Cay you will find an area close to shore which has good protection and easy seas. Holding is good in a sand-mud bottom, and a yacht drawing up to 7 feet can find overnight shelter here. Of course, the less you draw the farther in you can squeeze. Approach with caution and leave the island close at hand as the bottom shoals rapidly to the north at the head of the Bay.

ROAD HARBOR is the major commercial centre in the British Virgin Islands. The largest town in the British complex, Roadtown, is located here with assorted hotels, food stores, grog shops, restaurants and the like. Fresh food is quite expensive and quite limited compared to the sophisticated supplies found in St. Thomas. Yacht servicing including water, ice, fuel, etc. can be obtained at Tortola Yacht Services located just under Fort Burt on the western side of the harbor. They have a dock where you can tie up temporarily to take on supplies, clear customs, etc. Road Harbor is exposed for the most part to the prevailing easterly trade winds and is therefore not a particularly comfortable anchorage. During the winter when the winds are blowing north of east, however, the seas tend to ease somewhat. The most comfortable anchorage in this harbor is just off the Tortola Yacht Services dock. Use extreme caution when approaching this anchorage as a shallow sand bank extends about 150 yards to the northwest of Burt Point and is difficult to see because of the cloudy water. On rounding Burt Point it is best to continue on a heading for the main town docks until past the first line of moorings off the Tortola Yacht Services dock. At this point start rounding slowly up to port behind these moorings. Drop your hook anywhere in this area or continue on to the dock. When selecting your anchorage, be careful of another shoal area to the northwest. This very small spot is only 4 feet deep and difficult to see. Naturally, the closer you can anchor to the Tortola Yacht Services dock the easier the sea conditions will be due to the increased protection afforded by Burt Point. Holding here is excellent in sand. Swimming is not too good.

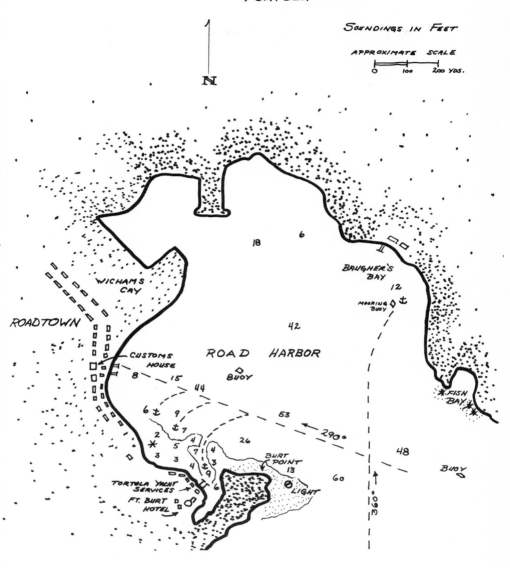

Road Harbor
Tortola

Soundings in Feet

Approximate Scale

0   100   200 YDS.

N

18   6

BAUGHER'S BAY

12

MOORING BUOY

WICHAMS CAY

ROADTOWN

42

ROAD HARBOR

CUSTOMS HOUSE

8   15   BUOY

44

6   9

7   53

290°

2   5   4   4

3   3   7   4   26   48

4   3   BURT POINT   BUOY

TORTOLA YACHT SERVICES   13

6   60

FT. BURT HOTEL   LIGHT

FISH BAY

Docking at the main town docks is not recommended for private yachts due to all the commercial traffic and the generally unsettled sea conditions. There is a temptation to do this when either entering or clearing because the Customs and Immigration offices are located in a large building just across the street. Don't be tempted. Either anchor out or stern-to at Tortola Yacht Services gas dock.

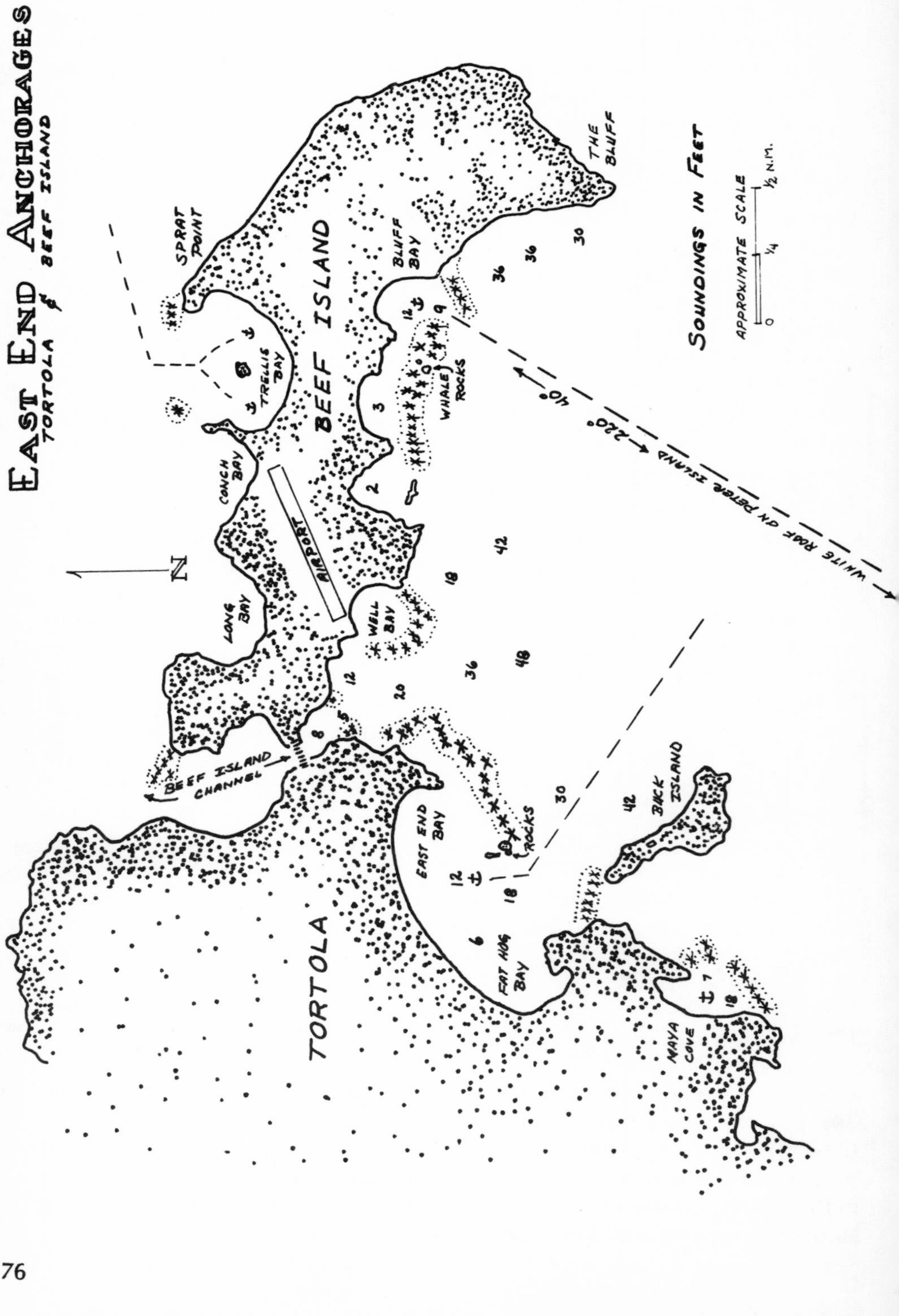

East End Anchorages
TORTOLA & BEEF ISLAND

SPRAT POINT

BEEF ISLAND

THE BLUFF

36

30

36

BLUFF BAY

14½
9

3

WHALE ROCKS

2

42

CONCH BAY

TRELLIS BAY

AIRPORT

LONG BAY

N

WELL BAY

18

36

48

12

20

BEEF ISLAND CHANNEL

8

5

x x
ROCKS

30

EAST END BAY

12

18

8

TORTOLA

FAT HOG BAY

6

NAYA COVE

7

18

JACK ISLAND

42

WHITE ROOF ON PETER ISLAND 220°

40°

SOUNDINGS IN FEET

APPROXIMATE SCALE

0   ¼   ½ N.M.

BAUGHERS BAY is another anchorage in Road Harbor which can sometimes be quite pleasant. It's location is on the eastern side of the harbor and can provide relatively calm conditions when the wind is north of east. A slight ground sea, however, almost always prevails. The best anchorage is just inside the large mooring buoy where holding is excellent in sand. The effects of the commercial traffic moving in and out of the harbor are not as apparent here. Swimming is good when the water is clear.

EAST END BAY, on the southeastern end of Tortola, is a lovely, quiet overnight anchorage. Holding is good in sand and grass, and the sea conditions are generally calm. The approach to this anchorage is straight forward offering a wide, deep entrance. The best anchorage is in the eastern side of the Bay just behind the entrance reef. After passing the rocks at the entrance simply bear off to starboard and drop your hook about 100 yards farther on. Stay well out from the head of the Bay as the bottom tends to shoal rapidly 2 to 3 hundred yards off shore. The town of East End is located here, but supplies and facilities are practically non-existant. Swimming is good in the anchorage.

THE NORTH COAST. On a nice day, when no ground sea is running, a trip down the north side of Tortola can be a pleasant experience. There are numerous coves and sandy beaches along this north shore but none can be recommended for overnight anchoring during the winter months because of their exposure to the north. It would seem that these spots would be relatively uncomfortable during the summer as well because of the unsettled conditions caused by the passing current and tidal streams. The route is generally clear of dangers except for the passage between Beef Island and the Camanoe Islands. Just north of Conch Bay, Beef Island, there is a reef right in the middle of the passage. It is best to pass north of this reef as another reef extends north from the headland between Conch Bay and Long Bay and can make navigation a bit tricky if you pass to the south. For the northern route around these reefs simply leave the southernmost points of both Great and Little Camanoe close on your starboard hand (20 to 30 yards). As you come abeam the southernmost point of Little Camanoe on your westerly heading, adjust your heading so that your bows are pointed directly toward the highest and closest visible mountain top on Tortola. This will be the 878 foot Lloyds, which is on the northeast corner of the island. Hold this heading until you are well by Little Camanoe and the sand-bar reef which extends south from its southwestern shore. Once clear of this hazard the remainder of the route down the north coast of Tortola is free of dangers. The passage between Guana Island and Tortola is clear with deep water extending very close to both shores. When sailing down the north coast of Tortola it is usually wise to stay rather well off shore in order to get clear air. This route is not recommended when the Rollers are coming in or when strong winds are blowing out of the northern quadrants.

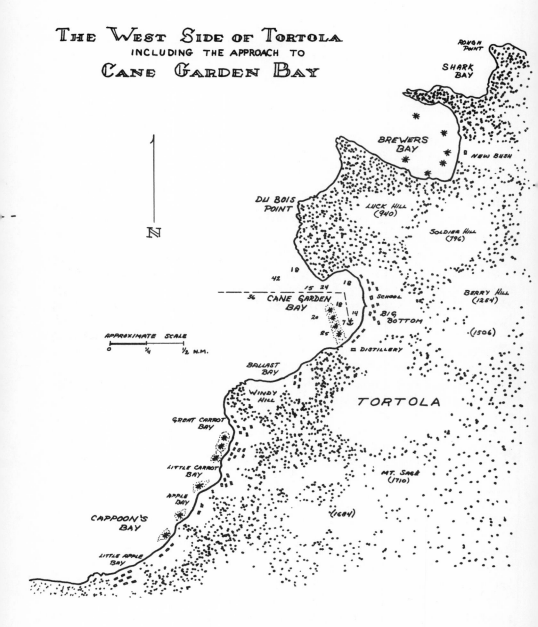

THE WEST SIDE OF TORTOLA
INCLUDING THE APPROACH TO
CANE GARDEN BAY

ROUGH POINT

SHARK BAY

BREWERS BAY

NEW BUSH

DU BOIS POINT

LUCK HILL (940)

SOLDIER HILL (796)

N

18

42

15 24

36   CANE GARDEN
BAY

SCHOOL

BERRY HILL (1254)

18

14

BIG BOTTOM

(1506)

20

7

25

DISTILLERY

APPROXIMATE SCALE

0   ¼   ½ N.M.

BALLAST BAY

WINDY HILL

TORTOLA

GREAT CARROT BAY

LITTLE CARROT BAY

MT. SAGE (1710)

APPLE BAY

CAPPOON'S BAY

(1684)

LITTLE APPLE BAY

CANE GARDEN BAY. The west coast of Tortola contains one of the most beautiful bays in the entire Virgin Islands complex: Cane Garden Bay. Unfortunately this Bay cannot be recommended as an overnight anchorage during the winter months because the Rollers can make the area dangerous and untenable within a few short hours. During the summer months, however, it is an excellent overnight anchorage and well worth a visit. When approaching from the west, favor the northern side of the Bay as there is a reef which extends from the southern side almost three quarters of the way across the entrance. The passage between the northern side of the Bay and the reef is clear of dangers and about 15 feet deep. Once inside the reef you will find the best anchorage in the southern part of the Bay. Holding is excellent in sand and the sea conditions are generally calm. A lovely sand beach complete with a pleasant native community, a rum distillery, and lots of children extends the full length of the Bay. Swimming is superb.

Photo by Jay Stone

Bluff Bay, Beef Island

BEEF ISLAND

This is a small island only about three miles long and a half mile wide located just off the eastern shore of Tortola. The two islands are connected by a bridge which spans the Beef Island Channel. The small international airport situated here is the major commercial airport servicing the British Virgin Islands. LIAT, Prinair and other carriers make scheduled stops from Puerto Rico and St. Thomas as well as from the Windward Islands. There are only two anchorages of any consequence on this island: Bluff Bay and Trellis Bay.

BLUFF BAY, on the south side of the island, is a small quiet anchorage offering good protection under normal conditions. When approaching this anchorage proceed with extreme caution as the entrance is narrow with dangerous coral heads and reefs on both sides. It is important to first identify the breaking reef on the eastern side of the Bay entrance and pass close to it (about 10 to 15 yards off) on a heading of approximately northeast. Once inside the reef alter course about 5 degrees to port and continue slowly toward the sandy beach at the head of the Bay. Be exceptionally wary of the reef which extends east from the Whale Rocks located to the west of the anchorage. This reef has scattered coral heads under 3 to 5 feet of water at it's eastern extreme which are difficult to see under anything but ideal conditions. Once inside of these hazards a yacht drawing 7 feet or less can anchor in comfort relatively close to shore. Holding is excellent in sand and the swimming is good. The sea conditions are generally calm. For those wishing to explore, there is an old plantation ruin in the underbrush just up from the beach. On leaving the anchorage favor the eastern side of the channel and head toward the white roof on Peter Island until well clear.

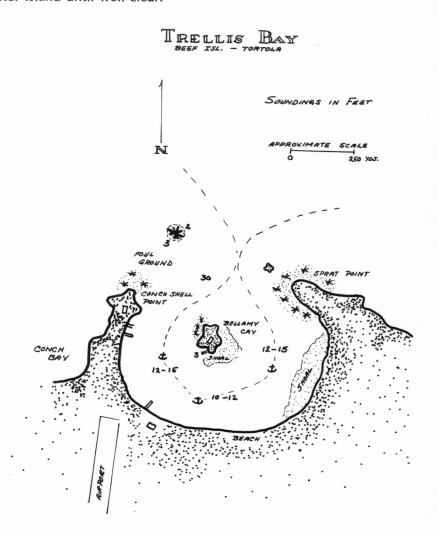

TRELLIS BAY
BEEF ISL. — TORTOLA

HIGHEST
POINT

IS BAY

Photo by Jay Stone

Passage Between Beef Isl. & the Camanoes

TRELLIS BAY is the largest and best known anchorage at Beef Island. Though open to the north, this Bay offers excellent protection under almost all conditions. Yachts may anchor on either side or in the lee of Bellamy Cay. Holding is good in sand, mud and grass, and the sea conditions are generally calm. On approaching from the east be sure to stand clear of the rock which is just above the water off the eastern point of the Bay. When approaching from the north or west be extremely careful of the foul ground which extends out from Conch Shell Point. Also, approximately 200 yards north and slightly to the east of Conch Shell Point there is a nasty little reef which lies about 3 feet below the surface of the water. A passage may be made between this reef and Conch Shell Point, though not recommended because of the difficulty in identifying the reef and it's outcroppings. The best procedure when passing this reef is to stand well to the east or north until clear. Bellamy Cay, located in the centre of the Bay, may be circumnavigated comfortably by yachts drawing 9 feet or less. Caution must be taken, however, when anchoring or passing to the east of the Cay as a shoal extends from both the shore and the Cay. The remainder of the Bay is clear of dangers except for a small reef which extends a short distance from the northwestern side of the Cay. Swimming is good and there are numerous possibilities for exploration both ashore and by dinghy. A guest house with a bar is located on Bellamy Cay, where meals can sometimes be had by prior reservation.

MARINA CAY

Marina Cay is a small island lying just south of Scrub Island and to the east of Great Camanoe. With these larger islands to the north and the Marina Cay reef extending to the east and south, the anchorage off the southwestern shore of the Cay offers good protection under practically all conditions. The approach to this anchorage from the north and northeast is clear of dangers as long as care is taken to stay well away from the reef which extends east from the northeast corner of the Cay. The channel between Great Camanoe and Scrub Island is clear of hazards though there are small reefs which extend a short distance from both shores; just stay more or less in mid-channel. When approaching from the south or southeast care must be taken to identify and pass well clear of the reef

Marina Cay, B.V.I.

Passage from Marina Cay to North Coast of Tortola

HIGHEST
POINT

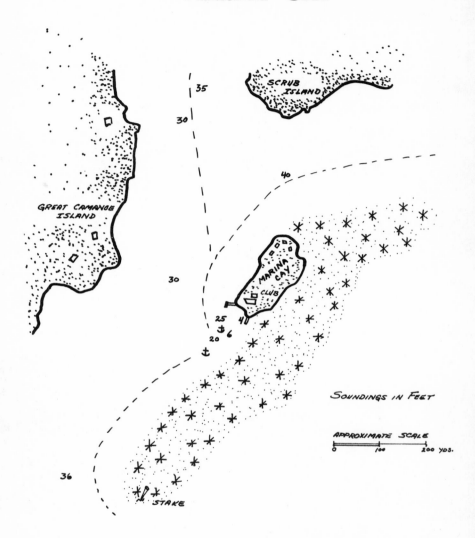

which extends approximately 500 yards to the south-southwest from the Cay. The reef is usually just awash and can be difficult to see at times. Identify and pass well clear of the stake which marks the southermost extreme of the reef and continue up along the inside channel to the anchorage. Holding is excellent in deep sand, sea conditions are generally calm and the swimming is superb. The proprietors of Marina Cay maintain several moorings for visiting yachtsmen and usually come out in a skiff to greet and direct you. The Club itself has an informal bar which is open to all. Meals and rooms are available by prior reservation. Limited supplies of fuel and water can usually be obtained here in an emergency. This is one of my favorite anchorages.

HIGHEST POINT

Photo by Jay Stone

Marina Cay & Passage

Marina Cay Reef

Photo by Jay Stone

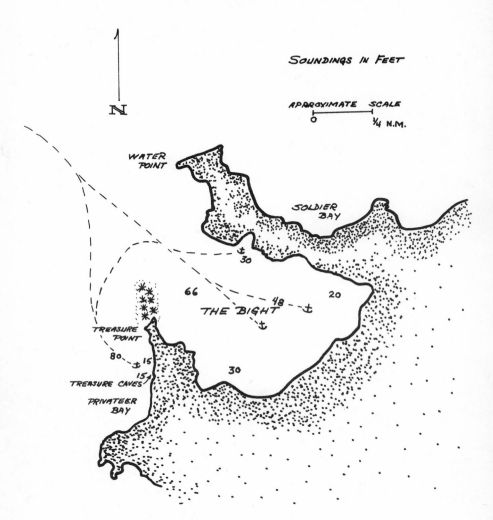

NORMAN ISLAND

Lying just 3 miles to the east of St. John, this island is reputed to be the famous "Treasure Island" immortalised in Robert Louis Stevenson's work of the same name. A camp site where the author is said to have lived while he was writing the work is said to be located on the beach at the head of The Bight.

THE BIGHT is a very large and quiet bay located on the northwest corner of the island which offers good protection under almost all conditions. Holding is excellent in sand and the sea conditions are generally calm. The approach is open and clear of hazards except for a reef which extends north for about 200 yards from Treasure Point. An anchorage may be found almost anywhere in this bay, though I prefer going right up to the head of the bay and anchoring about 50 yards off the beach. Just to the south of Treasure Point on the west side of the island are three caves known as the 'treasure caves". Rumour has it that not too many years ago quite a fortune was found in the wall of one of these caves. All three of these caves can be entered by dinghy under normal conditions. Yachts can be anchored on the narrow shelf which runs along this shore. It is a lovely lunch and afternoon stop, but not recommended for overnight anchoring. Swimming is good, though you'll usually see a lot of barracuda about.

PETER ISLAND

Peter Island, located just north of Norman Island and slightly to the east, has several anchorages of interest along its northern shore.

LITTLE HARBOR, the westernmost anchorage on the island, is also the most frequented by visiting yachtsmen. The entire western end of the island including Little Harbor is owned by Percy Chubb of marine insurance fame. His home is located on the northeastern bluff overlooking the anchorage. This is a deep anchorage which affords good protection under most conditions. Holding is excellent in sand, the sea conditions are generally calm and swimming is good. Since the land is privately owned, it is advisable to obtain permission prior to going ashore. Because of the topography of the land surrounding this anchorage, the wind tends to swirl at night which can cause yachts to come against one another, foul their anchors, etc. A stern anchor is therefore advisable for a worry-free night.

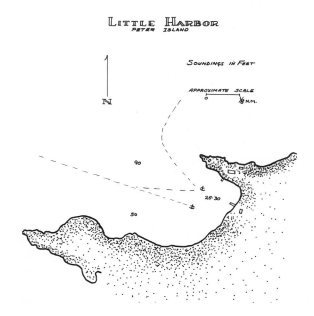

LITTLE HARBOR
PETER ISLAND

SOUNDINGS IN FEET

APPROXIMATE SCALE

N

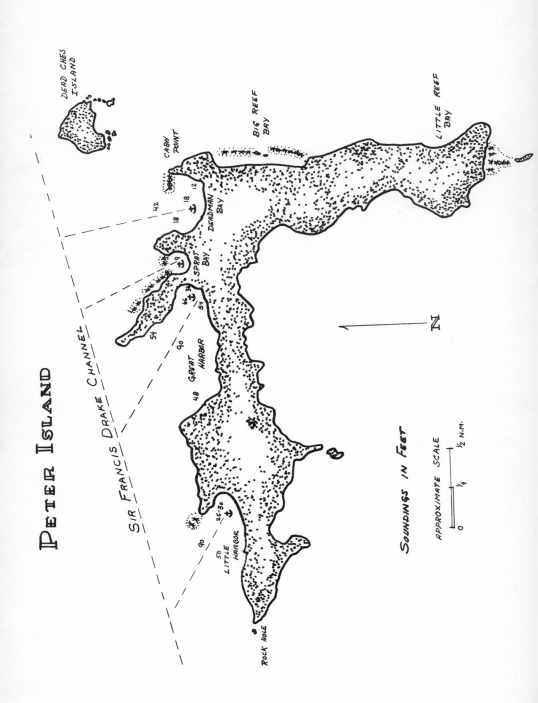

Peter Island

Sir Francis Drake Channel

Dead Ches Island

Cabey Point

Big Reef Bay

Little Reef Bay

Deadman Bay

Sprat Bay

Great Harbor

Little Harbor

Rock Hole

42
18
18
12
44 34
54
54
90
48
90
50
25-30

N

Soundings in Feet

Approximate Scale

0   ¼   ½ N.M.

Photo by Jay Stone

Spratt Bay & Deadman Bay

GREAT HARBOR, the largest bay on the north coast of the island, offers good protection but can only be recommended for yachts carrying ample amounts of chain rather than nylon anchor rope, because of the depth of the water. The best anchorage is in the southeastern corner of the bay where holding may be found in sand. One or two of the smaller cruise ships use this harbor to disgorge their passengers, who swarm ant-like over the surrounding hills to the less accessible sandy beaches and coves.

SPRAT BAY, lying between Great Harbor and Deadman Bay, is a small but comfortable overnight anchorage. The entrance is narrow and should be approached with caution. There is a reef extending west from the eastern mouth of the bay which is generally awash and easy to identify. Just behind this reef there is a concrete pier where yachts drawing 7 feet or less can anchor stern-to. The remainder of the bay is clear of dangers and yachts drawing 6 feet or less can anchor quite close to shore. Holding is good in sand and mud; the sea conditions are calm; protection is excellent. Swimming is fair, the water being usually more clear in the western part of the bay. All things considered, this is a rather pleasant anchorage . . . if you don't mind the chickens and the construction work.

DEADMAN BAY, on the northeastern end of the island, is generally acknowledged as one of the most beautiful bays in the Virgin Islands. With its crystal clear water and lovely, sandy beach backed by a palm grove, it looks like a picture out of a travel brochure. Unfortunately this lovely bay cannot be recommended as an overnight anchorage during the winter

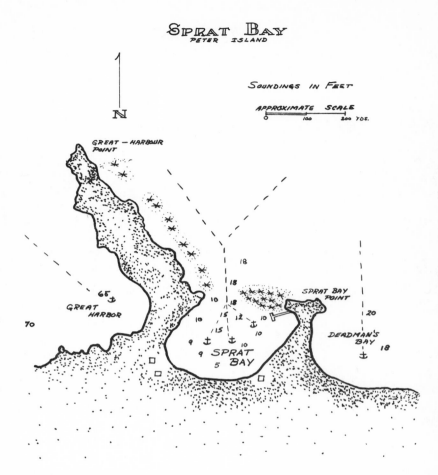

SPRAT BAY
PETER ISLAND

N

SOUNDINGS IN FEET

APPROXIMATE SCALE
0   100   200 YDS.

GREAT — HARBOUR
POINT

GREAT
HARBOR

65

70

GREAT
HARBOR

18

18

10

18

15 12   10

10

15

10

9

9   SPRAT

5   BAY

SPRAT BAY
POINT

20

DEADMAN'S
BAY

18

months because of it's vulnerability to the Rollers which can come in without warning and make the anchorage untenable. Holding is good in sand. A slight ground sea is almost always experienced in this anchorage, but, nevertheless, it is a wonderful lunch and afternoon stop. We understand that a hotel complex is about to be built here . . . (sigh).

SALT ISLAND

Salt Island, which is just east of Peter Island and Dead Chest, has a small settlement on it's northern shore who's inhabitants derive part of their living from working the salt pond that lies behind the settlement. The settlement is located in a shallow bight which shows quite an attractive beach when viewed from a distance. On closer examination, however, both the beach and the village shacks become less attractive. An anchorage can be found just off this beach under normal conditions for those interested in an afternoon's exploration or just lunch and a swim. Holding is good in sand. A slight ground sea is usually experienced even under the calmest conditions. This is not recommended as an overnight anchorage.

Deadman's Bay, Peter Island

Salt Island, North Coast

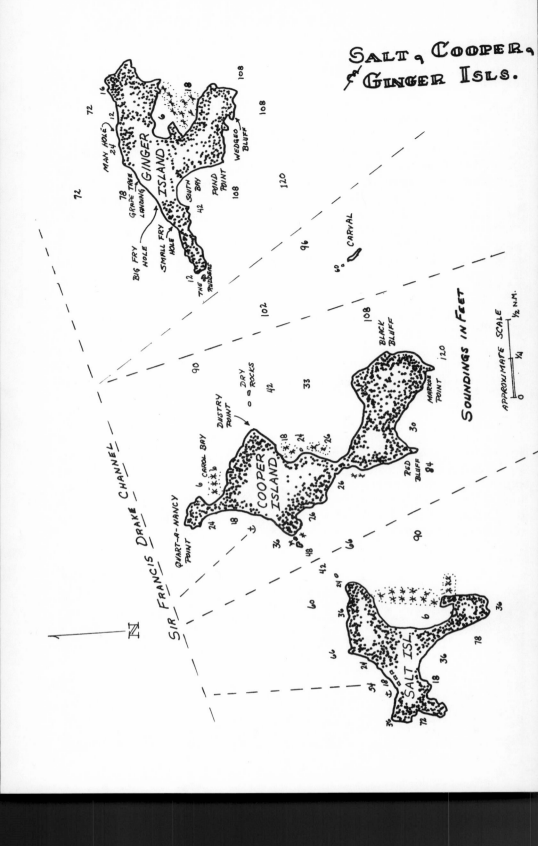

SALT, COOPER, GINGER ISLS.

GINGER ISLAND

MAN HOLE 24
72
16
12
9
18
108
108
108
WEDGO BLUFF
POND POINT
108
120
96
CARVAL
60

GRAPE TREE LANDING
78
BIG FRY HOLE
SMALL FRY HOLE
SOUTH BAY
42
12
THE TRIGONS

SIR FRANCIS DRAKE CHANNEL
N

72

102

90
DRY ROCKS
DUSTRY POINT
42
33
108
BLACK BLUFF
120
MARROW POINT
30

CARAL BAY
6
18
24
26
COOPER ISLAND
84
RED BLUFF
26

QUART-A-NANCY POINT
24
18
36
48
42
66
90
60

24
36
6
36

66
24
18
36
78

54
18
SALT ISL.
72
36

SOUNDINGS IN FEET

APPROXIMATE SCALE
0   ¼   ½ N.M.

PASSAGE between SALT ISLAND & COOPER ISLAND

When approaching this passage from the north proceed carefully as there are rocks and reefs extending from both islands at the narrowest part of the passage. Favor the eastern side of the channel, leaving the exposed rocks off the point on Cooper Island close at hand (about 20 to 30 yards). Once through this narrow spot the channel widens and no further dangers will be encountered.

COOPER ISLAND

Cooper Island has seen a great deal more development than either of her neighbors. There are a number of vacation homes already built here and several more presently being completed. There is an anchorage of sorts located in the lee of Quart-a-Nancy Point on the northwestern side of the island. Because of it's exposure to the north, this anchorage is not recommended for overnight stays during the winter months. The approach is open and clear of hazards. The best anchorage area under normal conditions seems to be in the lower part of the bay just inside the southern tip. A slight ground sea is almost always experienced. Holding is good in sand.

PASSAGE between COOPER & GINGER ISLANDS

This passage is open and unobstructed except for the Dry Rocks which extend east from Dustry Point on Cooper Island and the Carval Rock which is situated almost in the center of the passage just a half mile to the east of Black Bluff on Cooper Island. The remainder of the passage is clear of dangers.

GINGER ISLAND

Ginger Island is presently uninhabited and offers no safe anchorage for visiting yachtsmen. There is a bay on the east side of the island which has a 6-foot deep entrance through the reef and could offer good protection. Unfortunately, however, when the prevailing winds are blowing strongly out of the east-southeast this entrance becomes very dangerous and quite impossible to use. It can therefore not be recommended as an anchorage at the present time.

Photo by Jay Stone   **Bay East Side of Ginger Isl.**

93

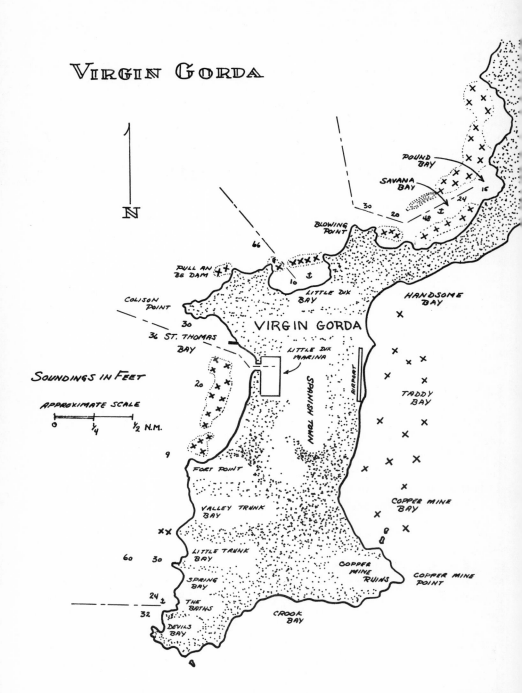

Virgin Gorda

POUND
BAY

SAVANA
BAY

30   20   48

24

16

BLOWING
POINT

PULL AN
BE DAM

66

XXX

10

LITTLE DIX
BAY

HANDSOME
BAY

COLISON
POINT

30

36 ST. THOMAS
BAY

VIRGIN GORDA

LITTLE DIX
MARINA

SPANISH TOWN

AIRPORT

TADDY
BAY

Soundings in Feet

Approximate Scale

0   ¼   ½ N.M.

20

9

FORT POINT

VALLEY TRUNK
BAY

XX

60   30

LITTLE TRUNK
BAY

SPRING
BAY

24

32

THE
BATHS

DEVILS
BAY

COPPER MINE
BAY

COPPER
MINE
RUINS

COPPER MINE
POINT

CROOK
BAY

The Baths

VIRGIN GORDA

Virgin Gorda is one of the largest of the British Virgin Islands and also one of the most beautiful. From the unusual giant boulders piled around the southern tip to the flat middle area and the high, lovely mountains in the northern section, it is certainly an island of contrast. Though it is the second most populated island in the British group, it has not been noticeably affected by the development mania which has enveloped Tortola. Lovely beaches abound, and some of the finest anchorages in the entire Virgin Islands complex are to be found around it's shores. The exclusive Little Dix Bay resort is presently the only hotel of any consequence on the island. Spanish Town is the major port of commerce and is located along the edge of St. Thomas Bay on the western side of the island.

THE BATHS, a phenomenal pile of huge boulders located on a lovely beach in a small open bay on the western side of the island, derives its name from the crystal clear salt water pools which are formed in the sand at the base of the pile. Great fun can be had climbing over the boulders and exploring the area. The bay is easy to spot from seaward. Simply set a course for the southern tip of the island. Within 2 miles of the western shoreline a string of lovely sand beaches can be clearly identified stretching northward along the coast. The second sand beach to the north of the island's southern tip is your destination. The pile of boulders in the southern corner of the beach is "The Baths". Approach the bay with caution and anchor 75-100 yards off the beach in a depth of about 25 to 35 feet. Check your anchor carefully as there are numerous coral heads about which could easily foul your anchor or saw through a nylon anchor line. A ground sea is almost always encountered here and can become very uncomfortable as well as dangerous during the times of the Rollers. If poor sea conditions exist, it is better to postpone your visit until another time or tie up at the Little Dix Marina in St. Thomas Bay and hire a jeep for a visit by land. This bay is definitely not recommended as an overnight anchorage during any time of the year. Swimming and snorkeling are excellent.

SPANISH TOWN

Spanish Town is a rather sleepy spot and a bit scattered about. Very limited supplies may be found here. The population is sparse with a good percentage working for Little Dix Bay. There is a pub called Lord Nelson's, which can sometimes be fun. Across the island from Spanish Town are some ruins of an old copper mine. A native boy will lead you there for a coin or two, or you can find your own way by walking over to the eastern shore and turning south. After climbing a few boulders you will spot the stack of the copper works ahead. This is a long walk over rough ground so take something to drink and wear old clothing. Taxis are available in the town for trips to The Baths or tours around the island.

ST. THOMAS BAY is the main anchorage for Spanish Town and the Little Dix Bay resort. A lovely marina is just being completed in the salt pond at the head of the Bay. This marina, built and operated by Little Dix, should prove to be one of the finest in the islands. Dockage will be available for approximately 100 yachts with several slips accommodating 100 footers. At the time of printing the marina was not yet open and no channel markers had been laid. For those wishing to use the facility it would be wise to either contact Little Dix prior to arriving for information, or (if you're already there) proceed to the dock at the head of the Bay and get directions from a local. Be wary of the reef to the south of the dock.

Photo by Jay Stone   **Little Dix Bay**

Little Dix Marina

Alternatively an anchorage may be found 50 yards or so to seaward and slightly to the north of this dock. Because little or no protection is available from the Rollers, this cannot be recommended as an overnight anchorage during the winter months. Holding here is good in sand in a depth of 20 to 30 feet. A slight ground sea is generally experienced throughout the year.

LITTLE DIX BAY, located about ½ mile to the northeast of Colison Point, is the site of the Little Dix Bay resort, another lovely Rockefeller development. The Bay has a beautiful sand beach running its full length and an outer reef which offers some protection for yachts. The hotel management, though very friendly and receptive to visiting yachtsmen, would prefer yachts using the marina in St. Thomas Bay. This is understandable inasmuch as the Little Dix Bay anchorage is off a lee shore and all waste from the yachts tends to wash up on the beach. The general conditions are not too comfortable here anyway with an unpleasant ground sea experienced throughout most of the year. The approach through the reef is toward the western tip of the Bay between a rock located just out from the point and the remainder of the reef to the east. Once inside the Bay there is a wide channel about 2 fathoms deep between the reef and the beach. This area is free of dangers with the best anchorage about half way up the Bay to the east. Holding is generally poor in shallow sand and the open aspect of the Bay to the north makes it a risky anchorage during the winter months. Good meals may be obtained ashore by prior reservation.

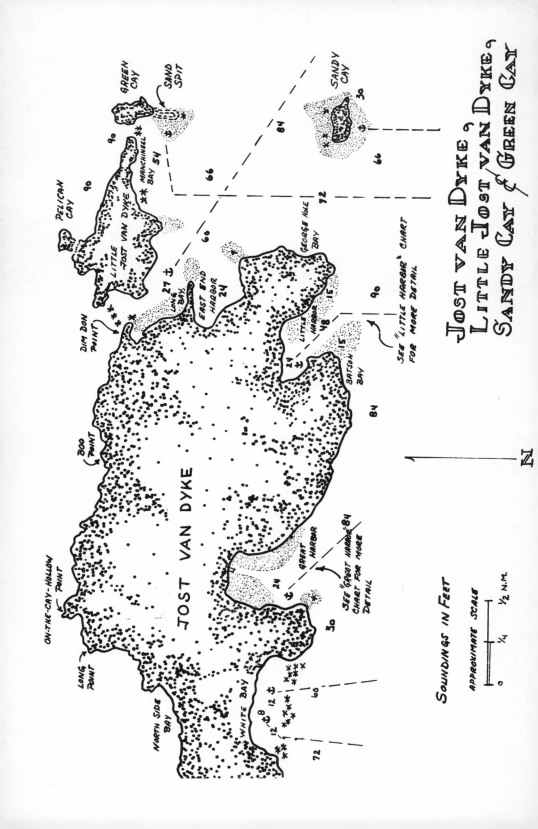

JOST VAN DYKE,
LITTLE JOST VAN DYKE,
SANDY CAY & GREEN CAY

SOUNDINGS IN FEET

APPROXIMATE SCALE

0   ¼   ½ N.M.

N

Savana Bay

SAVANA BAY, located just northeast of Little Dix, is reputed to be a comfortable anchorage under almost all conditions. To enter this Bay leave Blowing Point about 20 to 30 yards to starboard on a heading of east. Once inside follow the reef carefully for about 100 yards staying more or less in mid-channel. Don't venture too close to the shore as there are scattered coral heads and small reefs to be found in that direction. A good anchorage may be made either in Savana Bay or Pound Bay. Holding is good in sand. The sea conditions are generally calm though this anchorage cannot be recommended for overnight stays during the months of the Rollers. Swimming is excellent.

JOST VAN DYKE

Jost van Dyke, located about three miles west-northwest of Tortola, is the fourth largest island in the British group. The main town, as such, is located at the head of Great Harbor. A customs agent can usually be found here for entering and clearing during normal working hours. His office is across the street from the dock. If nobody is around, check at Foxy's Bar. This is by far the most pleasant spot in the British Virgin Islands to undertake these formalities.

GREAT HARBOR, on the southern shore of the island, affords good protection under all normal conditions. The best anchorage is in the southwest corner of the bay just inside of Dog Hole Point. Proceed into the bay, being careful to keep well clear of the small reef which projects southeast from the Point. Once inside you will notice that the bay shoals rapidly to 3-4 feet with a narrow channel running through the shallows to a dock on the beach. It is unwise to anchor in this channel because native sloops use it during all hours of the day and night. Anchor just

GREAT HARBOR
JOST VAN DYKE

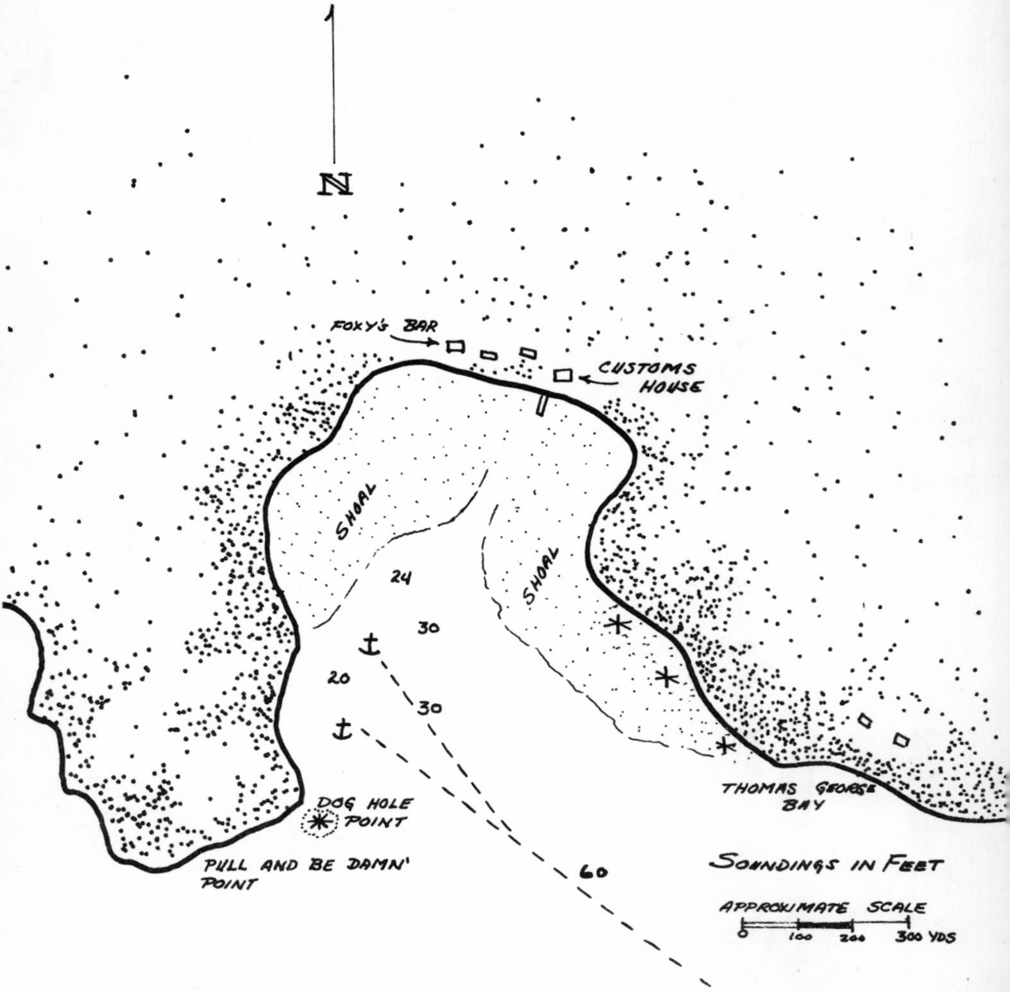

N

FOXY'S BAR

CUSTOMS HOUSE

SHOAL

SHOAL

24

30

20

30

DOG HOLE POINT

PULL AND BE DAMN' POINT

60

THOMAS GEORGE BAY

SOUNDINGS IN FEET

APPROXIMATE SCALE
0   100   200   300 YDS

south of the shoal area and close to the western shore. Holding is good in sandy mud and grass. The sea conditions are generally calm. For answers to all questions check at Foxy's Bar, located down the beach from the dock. Foxy's can be a fun place for an evening's entertainment. At the slightest hint of interest a native scratch band appears out of the woodwork. Ply them with a drink or two and the music goes on and on . . . Swimming is pleasant either from the boat or the beach.

Saba Rock

Anchorage Between Eustatia and Prickely Pear

Gorda Sound Looking East

Drakes Anchorage

LITTLE HARBOR, about a mile east of Great Harbor, is usually a quiet anchorage not frequently visited by yachtsmen. There are a few native homes along the northern shore, and I understand that a hotel complex is being considered for the eastern point. When entering Little Harbor stay in mid-channel as there are sand banks extending from each side of the entrance. Under normal conditions the channel is quite easy to identify. Once inside continue to the head of the bay where you will see on your port hand a tiny beach tucked into the corner. This corner is called "Careening Hole" and has 12 feet of water right up to the beach. It is a good idea to set a stern anchor here as the area is small and allows little swinging room. Conditions are generally calm and the holding is good in sand.

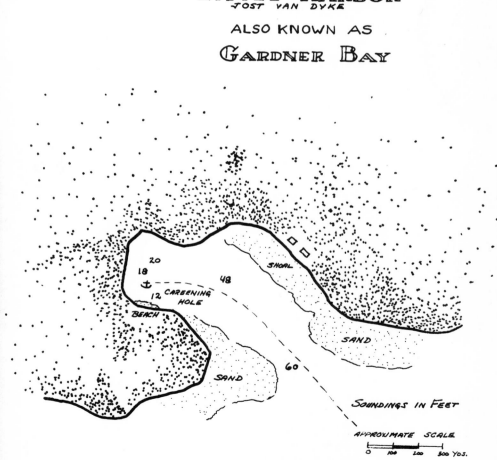

LITTLE HARBOR
JOST VAN DYKE

ALSO KNOWN AS

GARDNER BAY

20
18
48
12 CAREENING HOLE
SHOAL
BEACH
SAND
60
SAND

SOUNDINGS IN FEET

APPROXIMATE SCALE
0 100 200 300 YDS.

WHITE BAY, located just to the west of Great Harbor, has a lovely sandy beach which extends for the entire length of the Bay. The approach is tricky and should only be attempted under good sea conditions. The best passage through the reef is on the western side about 50 yards off the southwestern corner of the Bay. Approach with extreme caution and work your way slowly through the opening. Once inside be on the lookout for isolated coral heads which extend north from the reef. The best anchorage is in the middle of the Bay about 30-40 yards from the beach. Holding is good in sand, and the swimming is excellent. This is not a recommended overnight anchorage because of the generally unsettled sea conditions. If you wish local help for navigating this reef, check at Foxy's; the amount of assistance available for a bottle of rum (or gin) is truly remarkable.

LONG BAY, located on the northeastern side of Jost van Dyke, can be an interesting lunch, afternoon or overnight stop. When approaching Long Bay take care to avoid the sand bar which extends to the eastward of the southeasternmost point of the bay. A sand bar also extends along the entire head of the bay. You may anchor comfortably just off this bar in 20-30 feet of water. Holding is good in sand. Exploration by dinghy of the reef area which separates Little Jost van Dyke from the mainland can be well worth a visit for those interested in coral growth, small fish life, etc.

LITTLE JOST VAN DYKE

The man who designed the capitol building in Washington, D.C., was born on this island. There are two small beaches on the south shore which can be fun to explore and swim from when sea conditions allow. There are also several old ruins scattered about where the odd piece of crockery and empty Cherry Heering bottle can be discovered.

GREEN CAY

This little island lying just to the east of Little Jost Van Dyke, is well worth scrambling over; if only to visit the interesting miniature crater on its eastern side. The best anchorage is just on the sand bank which extends westward from the sand spit off the southern tip of the Cay. Holding is good and the swimming excellent. This is not a recommended overnight anchorage because of the uncomfortable ground sea which generally prevails.

SANDY CAY

This small cay is a lovely "desert island" type of spot for a lunch or afternoon stop. It is owned by the Rockefeller family who have endeavored to keep it as unspoiled as possible. There is a path running around the island which is interesting and fun to follow. The best anchorage is on the sand bank to the south-southwest of the island. Anchor about 50 yards from shore. Holding is good in sand. Because of its exposure and the prevailing ground seas, this is not a recommended overnight anchorage. Swimming and beach frolicking are both excellent here. A great picnic spot!

VIRGIN GORDA SOUND

Virgin Gorda Sound is probably the most magnificent piece of protected water in the entire Virgin Islands complex. There are two approaches to the Sound: the northern entrance and the western entrance.

THE NORTHERN ENTRANCE is between the northwest tip of Prickly Pear Island and Colquhoun Reef. When approaching this entrance from the west, keep the Reef 30 to 50 yards off the beam until the entrance is clearly identified. The reef is always either awash or breaking. Turn into the entrance to a heading of 180° favoring the western side of the channel as there is a small reef extending from the northwest corner of Prickly Pear Island. Once inside the reef Gorda Sound is relatively clear of hazards to the south and east. If, however, you are planning to anchor off Drake's Anchorage which is on the eastern shore of Mosquito Island, careful attention must be paid to the three small reefs which extend southwards from the southeasternmost end of Colquhoun Reef. To avoid these hazards maintain a heading of 180° with your bows pointed toward Gnat Point on Virgin Gorda until Anguilla Point bears due west or until the Seal Dog Islands drop behind the point. Then turn to a westerly heading and carry on until Drake's Anchorage is approximately due north. At this point you may consider yourself clear of the hazards and continue directly to the anchorage. This northern entrance to the Sound has no less than 20 to 30 feet of water and is open even in the heaviest sea conditions.

THE WESTERN ENTRANCE, which is a narrow passage between the southern tip of Mosquito Island and Anquilla Point, should be approached with caution. Heavy ground seas have frequently been known to break across the entire entrance. Under these conditions it is unwise to attempt a passage. Under normal conditions, however, a yacht drawing 6 feet or less can comfortably negotiate this entrance with little trouble. On approaching the entrance be especially wary of the reef which extends south from the southwestern point of Mosquito Island. The outermost limit of this reef can be identified under normal conditions because it is always awash and sometimes breaking. Leave this reef approximately 30 yards off the port beam as you approach the entrance on a heading of 90°. Stay in mid-channel until just inside Anguilla Point. Yachts drawing over 5 feet must then bear away either to the northeast or to the south-east to avoid a lump of sand located in mid-channel. This is the shallowest part of a sand bar which runs across the entrance. There is a minimum of 6 feet of water on either side of this lump. Once inside of this 5-foot shallow the Sound deepens to 20 feet or more. I have found

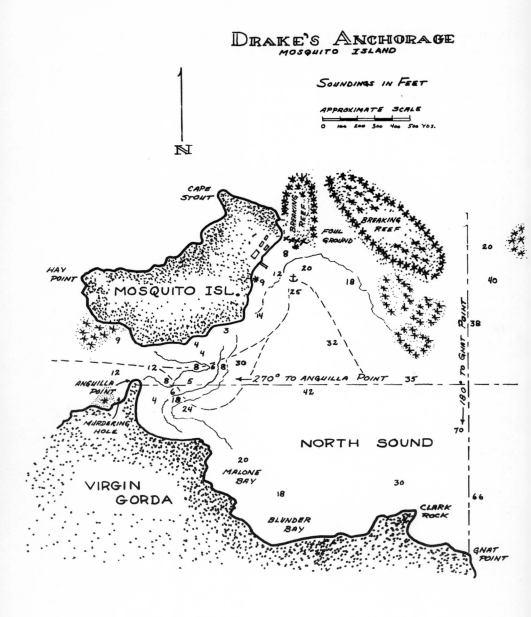

DRAKE'S ANCHORAGE
MOSQUITO ISLAND

SOUNDINGS IN FEET

APPROXIMATE SCALE

0   100   200   300   400   500 YDS.

N

CAPE STOUT

BREAKING REEF

FOUL GROUND

BREAKING REEF

20

HAY POINT

MOSQUITO ISL.

40

38

9

3

8   12   20

9

25

18

14

4

32

12   8   6   8   30

270° TO ANGUILLA POINT   35

8   5

ANGUILLA POINT

6   42

4   18

MURDERING HOLE

24

70

180° TO GNAT POINT

NORTH SOUND

20

MALONE BAY

30

VIRGIN GORDA

18

66

CLARK ROCK

BLUNDER BAY

GNAT POINT

that the southeastern route around the shallow is the most reliable because the commercial boats that put into Gun Creek use it and tend to keep it open. This channel can easily be seen in calm sea conditions. If continuing eastward from the entrance, be careful to stand well clear of the three small reefs which extend south from the southeastern end of Colquhoun Reef (see: NORTHERN ENTRANCE).

DRAKE'S ANCHORAGE: is the name of a small guesthouse-restaurant facility located on the eastern shore of Mosquito Island. The anchorage itself is pleasant and usually quiet. Colquhoun Reef and it's extremities provide excellent protection under almost all conditions. Holding is good in sand. All yachts regardless of draft can anchor within 50 yards of shore just out from the dock. Swimming and snorkeling are excellent.

GUN CREEK is the only settlement in the Sound, though small holiday homes and guesthouses are beginning to appear on every side. Very limited supplies are available here. Once ashore, a climb to the top of the hill is rewarding with views of the lovely South Sound as well as some of the other Virgin Islands including Anegada to the north. The approach to this anchorage is open and clear of dangers. Anchor 30 to 50 yards seaward of the dilapidated pier at the head of the bay. This is generally a calm anchorage with good holding in sandy mud and good protection under most conditions. Swimming is fair, but there are a lot of better places close by.

ROBIN'S BAY, about three quarters of a mile east of Gun Creek, is a pleasant and comfortable anchorage when the wind is blowing east to south. This anchorage, however, does tend to become unsettled when the wind is north of east. The approach is open and clear of hazards. The best anchorage is along the southeast shore about 30 yards or so off in 10 feet of water. Holding is good in sand. Swimming is good.

BIRAS CREEK which is three quarters of a mile east of Robin's Bay affords excellent protection under almost all conditions. Holding is good in sand and the sea conditions are generally calm. When approaching this anchorage from the west, keep a sharp eye open for Oyster Rock which lies about 200 yards off the shore just to the north of Camelia Point. This Rock is just below the surface and cannot always be clearly seen. Once clear of Oyster Rock the approach holds no further dangers. If the weather has been dry you may anchor comfortably as far up the Creek as you wish, but during the wet season stay well out. The marsh at the head of the Creek is breeding ground for mosquitoes.

SABA ROCK, which divides the channel between Prickly Pear Island and the mainland, offers a lovely anchorage off its western shore under normal conditions. The approach to this anchorage from the west is clear of dangers. Anchor along the western shore, but be sure to either allow for ample swinging room or put out a stern anchor. The changing tidal stream running through the cut has been known to set the unwary right against the Rock. The sea conditions are generally calm and the holding is good in sand. Swimming is excellent. This anchorage is usually bug-free under the dampest conditions.

PRICKLY PEAR ISLAND offers a pleasant anchorage on a sandy shelf about half way down its western side. This shelf extends two to three hundred yards off shore. The approach is clear except for one or two coral heads located about 400 yards north of Vixin Point and about 150 yards from shore. Holding is good in sand and the sea conditions are generally calm under normal conditions. Swimming is good.

EUSTATIA SOUND

The approach to Eustatia Sound should be attempted only under ideal conditions and with extreme caution by yachts drawing less than 6 feet. Enter on the south side of Saba Rock on a heading of 60°. Maintain this heading until the deeper water of the Sound is reached. Caution should be exercised as there are reefs and rocks along the route which must be avoided. The water is usually clear, so all hazards can be spotted well in advance. For the best possible spotting conditions wait until the sun is overhead and slightly behind you. Once by the reefs and coral heads which abound along the western side, the Sound is relatively clear of hazards except for a few isolated rocks and reefs in the eastern section. The main body of the Sound is well protected by an outer reef and offers good swimming and excellent snorkeling.

DEEP BAY, located in the southwestern corner of Eustatia Sound, is a good overnight anchorage under almost all condtions. The approach from the deep water of the Sound is clear of hazards with the exception of the rocks and small reefs which lie close to shore. A good anchorage may be found in sand and 10 feet of water well up into the Bay. Sea conditions are generally easy and holding is good in sandy mud.

EUSTATIA ISLAND. By far the easiest and safest approach to the anchorage between Prickly Pear and Eustatia Island is from the north. Simply pass Opuntia Point (on Prickly Pear) about 50 yards off the starboard beam on a heading of 150° and sail right on in. There are no hazards on this approach except for the reef which extends westward about 500 yards from Eustatia Island . . . just stay well away from it. Under ideal conditions there are several choices for a lunch or a swim stop in the area: off the beach on Prickly Pear, in the lee of Eustatia, etc. On a nice day under ideal conditions this is truly a delightful spot. It cannot, however, be recommended as an overnight anchorage during the winter because of its open aspect to the north. Holding is good in sand, and the swimming and snorkeling are excellent.

VIRGIN SOUND

The Virgin Sound is located between Eustatia and Necker Islands. The main body of the Sound is free of hazards, though extreme care must be taken to avoid the reefs which extend to the north of Eustatia Island as well as those which extend to the south of Necker Island. By maintaining a bearing of 270° on Mosquito Rock, a safe mid-channel passage through the Sound can be guaranteed. Because of its exposure to both

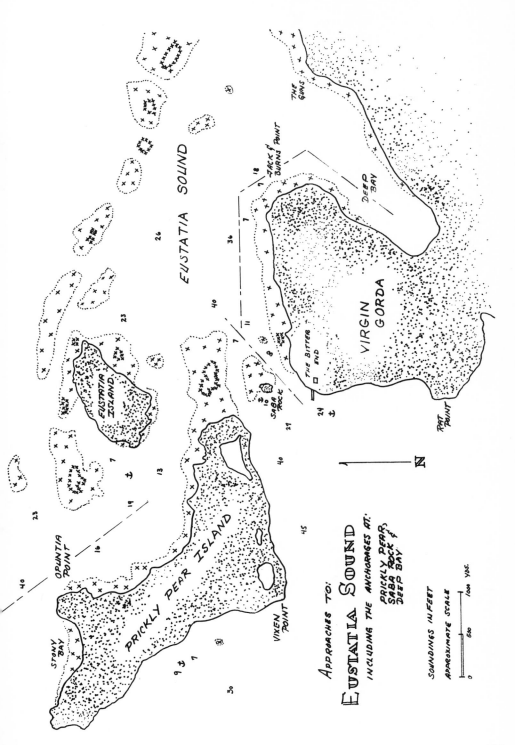

APPROACHES TO:

EUSTATIA SOUND

INCLUDING THE ANCHORAGES AT:

PRICKLY PEAR,
SABA ROCK &
DEEP BAY

SOUNDINGS IN FEET

APPROXIMATE SCALE

0   500   1000 YDS.

EUSTATIA SOUND

EUSTATIA ISLAND

PRICKLY PEAR ISLAND

OPUNTIA POINT

STONY BAY

VIXEN POINT

VIRGIN GORDA

THE BITTER END

SABA ROCK

JACK & BURNS POINT

DEEP BAY

THE GUNS

PAT POINT

N

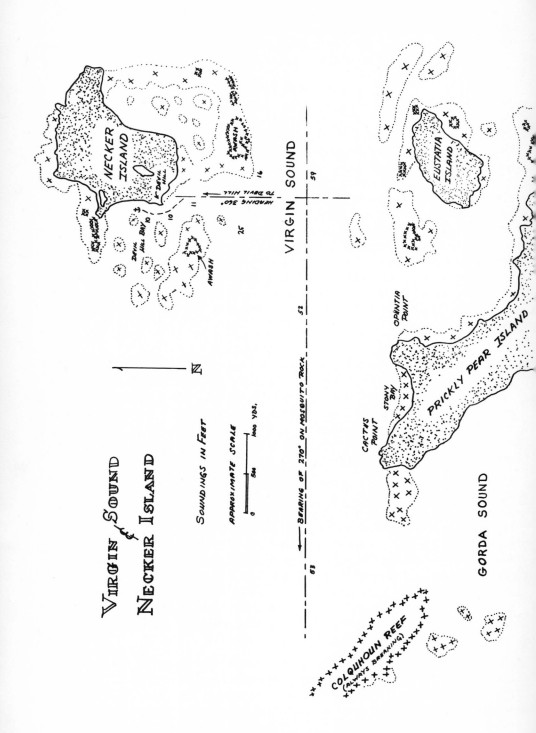

VIRGIN SOUND
&
NECKER ISLAND

SOUNDINGS IN FEET

APPROXIMATE SCALE

0   500   1000 YDS.

N

NECKER ISLAND

Mt DEVIL HILL

DEVIL HILL BAY

AWASH

HEADING 360° TO DEVIL HILL

VIRGIN SOUND

BEARING OF 270° ON MOSQUITO ROCK

EUSTATIA ISLAND

OPUNTIA POINT

PRICKLY PEAR ISLAND

CACTUS POINT

STONY BAY

GORDA SOUND

COLQUHOUN REEF
(ALWAYS BREAKING)

the north and the east, the Virgin Sound is not really a pleasant cruising area except under the occasional light sea and wind conditions which sometimes exist. The reefs to the north of Eustatia Island are difficult to identify even in ideal conditions, so proceed with care!

NECKER ISLAND

Necker Island, located on the north side of the Virgin Sound, is a lovely, uninhabited island which is fascinating because if its solitude as well as its interesting and beautiful beaches. The approach to Necker from Virgin Sound is relatively straight forward. When Necker Island bears due north you will notice a small rise of land known as Devil Hill on the southwest corner of the island which flattens out to the eastward. Approach this rise cautiously on a heading of north, being especially watchful for a small, isolated reef in the western part of the entrance. Anchor about 100 yards off the rocky shore directly below this small rise or bear off slightly to port and round the point picking your way carefully through the isolated coral heads. A good anchorage may be found just off the lovely beach in Devil Hill Bay. This is generally an unsettled anchorage and not recommended except under ideal conditions; and certainly not for overnight stays. Holding is good in sand. Swimming and snorkeling are excellent, but probably the most fun is exploring!

ANEGADA

Anegada is the northernmost as well as one of the largest of the Virgin Islands and is about 12 miles north-northeast of Virgin Gorda Sound. This island is totally different from the other Virgins in that the average height of the land is only 30 feet. Also the island is completely surrounded by a barrier reef which extends as much as three miles from shore. Needless to say, these combined conditions of low profile and dangerous reef demand careful and exacting navigation by the visiting yachtsman.

Until recently the island has been populated by only 300 or so natives who derived their living primarily from the sea. In 1968, however, the entire island was leased from the British Crown by Kenneth Bates, an English land developer who is presently building roads, docks, an airport, schools, hotels, homes, etc. in hopes of creating further development interest from outside sources. Mr. Bates can usually be found in or around his office at Setting Point, located on the south shore of the island toward the western tip. This location is strategically important because the only safe anchorage for the entire island is located here. Mr. Bates has wisely built his jetty on the tip of Setting Point and presently claims to be bringing in cargo barges drawing as much as 9 feet.

Needless to say, this island offers very interesting potential for development. There is a lovely, practically unbroken beach almost 22 miles in length which runs completely around the island. For those interested in snorkelling and diving there is unlimited opportunity and variety. Swimming, naturally, is excellent.

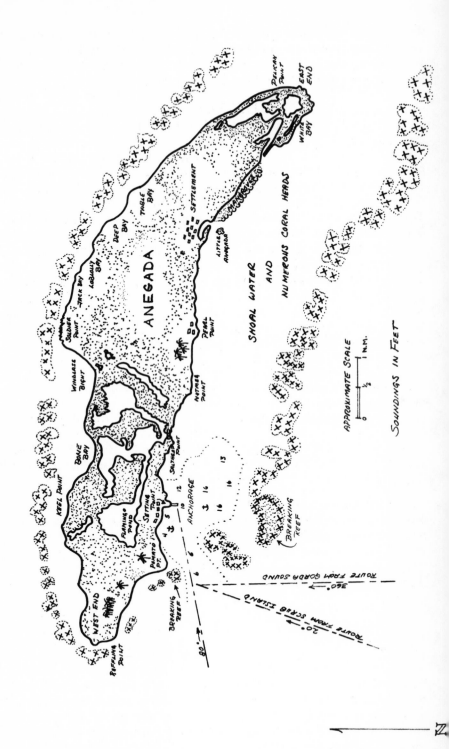

ANEGADA

ANEGADA

SOLDIER POINT · WINDLASS BIGHT · JACK BAY · ASBURY BAY · DEEP BAY · TABLE BAY · SETTLEMENT · LITTLE ANEGADA · MANGROVE · PELICAN POINT · EAST END · WHITE BAY

SHOAL WATER AND NUMEROUS CORAL HEADS

NUTMEG POINT · PENEL POINT · SALTHEAP POINT

BONE BAY · SETTING POINT ROAD · RUNNING POND · PAMATO PT. · WEST END · RUFFLING POINT · KEEL POINT

ANCHORAGE

BREAKING REEF

13
12   16
16   16
16
4 5
6
6
80'

BREAKING REEF

← 360'→ ROUTE FROM GORDA SOUND
20'↗ ROUTE FROM SCRUB ISLAND

APPROXIMATE SCALE
0   ½   1 N.M.

SOUNDINGS IN FEET

N

At the time of printing, food and water supplies were not available for visiting yachtsmen, though Mr. Bates has stated that these amenities will be forthcoming in the very near future.

APPROACH to the ANCHORAGE off SETTING POINT

The approach to this anchorage is straight forward enough for the experienced yachtsman providing, of course, that the following directions are carefully adhered to:

Depart from the easternmost point of Scrub Island on a heading of 20° (or the western entrance of Gorda Sound on a heading of 360°). Your course will be set toward Pomato Point on the western end of Anegada. The distance from Scrub Island to Pomato Point is 15 miles. Over half of that distance will be covered before you make your first landfall on Anegada. From Gorda Sound the distance is slightly more than 12 miles.

The first indication of land will be a cluster of palms well off the starboard bow. This is the palm grove at Pearl Point . . . maintain your heading. A short time later a single palm tree will emerge from the horizon almost dead ahead. This palm tree is located on the beach between West End and Pomato Point . . . maintain your heading. Almost immediately thereafter another clump of palms will emerge to the left of this single palm and another single palm will show itself just to the right of the first. This second, most easterly, palm is just inland from Pomato Point and is going to be your major piloting reference, so be sure to have it positively identified . . . maintain your heading.

As the beach begins to appear, adjust your heading (if necessary) so that you are sailing directly toward this Pomato Point palm. Your heading should be no less than 360° and no greater than 30°. Continue on until the end of the jetty off Setting Point bears 80°. Yachts drawing less than 6 feet may then turn to a heading of 80° and continue carefully toward the jetty. Those drawing 6 feet or more should not attempt this approach without more detailed information concerning the channel to the dock. At the time of printing this information was as yet not available.

There is a small reef just off Pomato Point which must be left to port on your heading of 80°. When passing abeam this reef be on the lookout for two coral heads which lie slightly to the east and are covered by only a few feet of water. These are the only obstructions in the channel, and once by them (you might not even see them) the course is clear to the jetty. Yachts drawing 5 feet or less may anchor well in the lee of Setting Point. Deeper draft vessels may anchor out from Setting Point or to the east where the water reaches a depth of 16 feet. This anchorage is almost a mile wide by a mile and a half long and provides excellent protection under practically all conditions. The seas are generally calm in the lee of Setting Point with a very light chop sometimes developing in the eastern anchorage. Holding is good in sandy mud and grass.

INDEX

INDEX TO CHARTS